In the Mouth of the Dragon

香港

Hong Kong—Past, Present and Future

Philip Geddes

CENTURY PUBLISHING CO.
LONDON
in association with TVS

First published in Great Britain in 1982 by
Century Publishing Co. Ltd, 76 Old Compton Street, London W1
ISBN 0 7126 0052 3
Photoset in Plantin by
Rowland Phototypesettng Ltd
Bury St Edmunds, Suffolk
Printed in Great Britain by
Hazell, Watson & Viney
Aylesbury
Book design by Jim Wire

ACKNOWLEDGEMENTS

This book came about as a result of a documentary series made for Television South. Many people in London and Hong Kong helped in the making of that series. I would like to thank James Dreaper, Nanette McLintock and their colleagues at the Hong Kong and Shanghai Bank; Cathay Pacific Airways; the Hong Kong Tourist Association; Kerry McGlynn, Ranjit Peiris and their colleagues in the Hong Kong Government Office in London; Alan Scott and the staff of the Government Information Office in Hong Kong. A special word of thanks is due to Christine Loh for all her help and encouragement; to the numerous people who went out of their way to help us in our work while we were in Hong Kong I must also give my heartfelt thanks.

I should also record my gratitude to my colleagues at TVS: Michael Blakstad, Director of Programmes, for his confidence in us; Bob Garratt, who was so good a guide to Hong Kong; Michael Rodd, Bob Franklin and Alan Griffiths, my editorial colleagues, whose energy and enthusiasm made working a pleasure; Roy Page and the others in the film crew, who nobly put up with a schedule that was diabolical; my secretary, Cathy Purchase, for so deftly interpreting the English of my manuscript; and all the backroom people at TVS who put so much into making a memorable series.

Photographs: Hong Kong harbour in 1850 courtesy of the Hong Kong and Shanghai Bank; William Jardine and James Matheson courtesy of Jardine Matheson; the Hong Kong Gold Market, Sir Murray MacLehose and Hong Kong by night courtesy of the Hong Kong Government; Hong Kong Land advertisement courtesy of Hong Kong Land Company. The other photographs were taken by TVS photographer Tony Nutley, Bob Franklin, Alan Griffiths and the author.

To my parents, with much love

CONTENTS

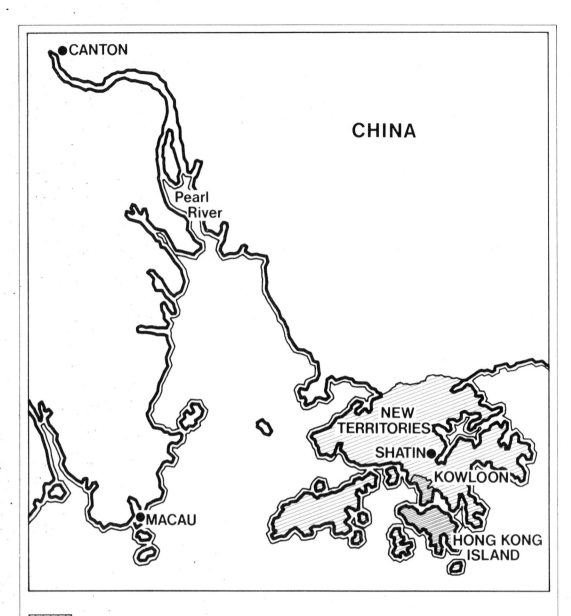

FOREWORD

As the last words of this book are being written, Sir Edward Youde is being sworn in as the twenty-sixth governor of the British Crown Colony of Hong Kong. By the time he retires, the great question mark hanging over Hong Kong will have been removed. China and Britain will have between them determined whether Sir Edward is to be the last of his line, or is to be succeeded by a twenty-seventh governor.

The lease on 90 per cent of Hong Kong's land area, the New Territories, expires on the 30 June 1997. The question of this lease will be the central problem of Sir Edward's governorship. This book is not intended as a lament for the last outpost of empire; it is an attempt to paint a portrait of an extraordinary society; one that is both dynamic and complex, and at the centre of the world's fastest growing region. It is a place where both problems and achievements are on a big scale. For those whose view is coloured by visions of cheap shirts and Chinese takeaways, I hope to show that there is a lot more to Hong Kong than that.

I have tried to let Hong Kongers speak for themselves in their own words. I apologise in advance to those who know Hong Kong much better than I for my interpretation of those words. For what it is worth, the following may serve as a warning to the reader. George Wingrove Cooke, *The Times* correspondent in China between 1857 and 1858 wrote home:

> I have always found the most eminent and candid Sinologues ready to agree with me as to the impossibility of the Western mind forming a conception of Chinese character as a whole. These difficulties occur, however, only to those who know the Chinese practically; a smart writer, entirely ignorant of the subject, might readily strike off a brilliant and antithetical analysis, which should leave nothing to be desired but Truth.

May 1982

CHAPTER ONE

THE TIME BOMB

In late 1981 a military truck driver took the wrong turning at the end of San Lau street in the village of Sha Tau Kok and drove his patrol of kilted British Highland troops into China by mistake. It's not a mistake he'd have made in any comparable confrontation point in Western Europe. But it was an easy one to make here—apart from an old and almost illegible sign, it's not easy to spot where Hong Kong ends and China begins.

Sha Tau Kok is a small village on the northern border of the British Crown Colony. It is to Hong Kong what Berlin is to Western Europe—the potential flashpoint, the place where communism and capitalism come face to face. But there the resemblance ends. There are no searchlights, no massive military formations, no divisions of tanks or squadrons of aircraft facing each other. The Highlanders who visited China by mistake received no more serious punishment than a cup of Chinese tea and polite directions out of China. In the village itself the border hardly exists. My guide, a colonel in charge of the Gurkha battalion currently policing the border, pointed with an elegant swagger stick at some nondescript stones alongside a ditch and announced, as if it were obvious, that this was the border.

Elsewhere it is a little more obvious. In formal terms the border is the north bank of the Shum Zhum river, but with supreme disregard for the niceties of politics, the river changes its course from time to time, annexing chunks of China to Hong Kong and vice versa.

Unlike the Iron Curtain of Europe, it's a remarkably open frontier. The border fence, twenty-six miles long, looks formidable until you realise it takes the average illegal immigrant from China about one minute flat to get through. They could of course save themselves even this amount of work by using one of the 150 gates in the fence. These are installed for the convenience of farmers who suddenly find that a piece of their land has changed country and is now in Hong Kong as opposed to China. Only three of the gates are guarded regularly; many stay open for most of the time. A massive tide of humanity moves backwards and forwards across the border.

There was a time when things were not so quiet. In 1967 when China was in the throes of its Cultural Revolution, those Highland soldiers would have found themselves prisoners in an undeclared war. The Red Guards, the activists of Mao Tse Tung's second revolution, fought British Gurkhas from rooftop to rooftop along San Lau Street. Man Kam To police station was converted into battle headquarters as sniping and an even more insidious

The old and the new—junks in the harbour and skyscraper blocks.

assault, non-stop propaganda through loudspeakers, bombarded its garrison.

Today all that is an unpleasant dream, something not to be mentioned in polite company. The policeman in charge of Sha Tau Kok, Chief Inspector Garth Burrows, notes the recent difference: 'Even two or three years ago people used to look through you as if you didn't exist. Now they look at you and you get the occasional smile.' The policeman's lot is a relatively happy one now but, like everyone else in Hong Kong, Burrows knows that the peace may be only temporary, that a looming political problem threatens the quiet of the border. If questioned, he laughs uneasily and replies that, 'the lease is the sixty-four million dollar question; and the one that no one can answer.'

Everything in Hong Kong comes back to 'the lease'. It's the fundamental reality of a place that knows it's living on a time bomb. For on 1 July 1997 90 per cent of the land area of Hong Kong—including the village of Sha Tau Kok—will revert to Chinese control. If the date sounds precise, it is just that—it says so in the lease.

The other 10 per cent of Hong Kong—the island and a small slice of flat land on the Kowloon peninsular—is leased to Britain in perpetuity. The main land area of the colony was leased in 1898 from China in order to give Hong Kong more land and greater security from attack. This part of Hong Kong was called the New Territories—a strangely impermanent name that has stuck, almost as if Britain knew it could never hang on to the land. It is now only fifteen years to the time when the New Territories must be handed back to China.

Psychologically, Hong Kong has in one respect already accepted that change. At the top end of Kowloon, near the airport, you'll find Boundary Road among all the Chinese road names. It's just what it suggests—the border between the part of Kowloon that is leased in perpetuity and the New Territories. Theoretically, on 1 July 1997 China will begin on the north side of Boundary Road. It is somewhat absurd since the north side looks like the south side and you couldn't run a border down the middle of the road. But the law states that this is to be the new frontier. Shops on the south side will be in Hong Kong, shops on the north side in China. Seeing Boundary Road makes one suspect that the whole lease question is some strange fantasy, a joke dreamed up by a Foreign Office official on a dull day.

For a tenant whose lease is running out, the British government seems remarkably unconcerned. Perhaps it is symbolic that when we asked to photograph the lease for our television series, it took the Foreign Office some time to work out what had been done with it. 'I'm not sure I even know where it is,' said one official on the Far Eastern desk. A few days later he came back to us in triumph, having discovered that it had been moved out to a vault near Kew Gardens for safekeeping during the Second World War.

It wouldn't be surprising if it had been lost. There's not much of it to lose and it looks more like a Victorian laundry list than a major document of state. Headlined on the front page in a rough, clerk's scrawl 'Convention for the Extension of Hong Kong', it's only four pages long. The most impressive part of it is the large Chinese imperial 'chop' or seal at the end. Its provisions are vague, announcing that the territory of Hong Kong is to extend as far as 'the attached map'. The map is unfortunately rather sketchy and not very accurate and it is only by tacit agreement that the border has now been defined as the north bank of the Shun Zhum river.

In fact the British don't ever seem to have taken the lease very seriously. One clause permits Chinese authority over Kowloon City to continue 'except so far as may be inconsistent with the military requirements for the defence of Hong Kong'. The British decided unilaterally to revoke this clause by an Order in Council on 27 December 1898, just a few months after the lease was granted. Kowloon City is now seen by Britain as administratively part of Hong Kong. No one asked the Chinese what they thought.

But it is on that scrap of paper that the future rests. If Britain's Foreign Office doesn't seem particularly concerned about the lease and its provisions, its implications are certainly important for the five and a half million inhabitants of Hong Kong. It is that scrap of paper, after all, which ensures the lifestyle and standard of living they enjoy today.

For Hong Kongers, the New Territories are not an abstraction on a map or an optional extra, they're a vital and integral part of the present and—more important—the future of Hong Kong. They comprise nine-tenths of the land area of a place that is strapped for space and represent the future in a personal and tangible way for millions of people—those who will

Convention for the Extension of Hongkong

Whereas it has for many years past been recognised that an extension of Hongkong territory is necessary for the proper defence and protection of the Colony,

It has now been agreed between the Governments of Great Britain and China that the limits of British territory shall be enlarged under lease to the extent indicated generally on the annexed map. The exact boundaries shall be hereafter fixed when proper surveys have been made by officials appointed by the two Governments. The term of this lease shall be ninety-nine years.

It is at the same time agreed that within the city of Kowloon the Chinese officials now stationed there shall continue to exercise jurisdiction except as far as may be inconsistent with the military requirements for the defence of Hongkong. Within the remainder of the newly-leased territory Great Britain shall have sole jurisdiction. Chinese officials and people shall be allowed as heretofore to use the road from Kowloon to Hsinan.

It is further agreed that the existing landing place near Kowloon city shall be reserved for the convenience of Chinese men-of-war, merchant and passenger vessels, which may come and go and lie there at their pleasure; and for the convenience of movement of the officials and people within the city.

When hereafter China constructs a railway to the boundary of the Kowloon territory under British control, arrangements shall be discussed.

It is further understood that there will be no expropriation or expulsion of the inhabitants of the district included within the extension, and that if land is required for public offices, fortifications, or the like official purposes, it shall be bought at a fair price.

If cases of extradition of criminals occur, they shall be dealt with in accordance with the existing treaties between Great Britain and China and the Hongkong Regulations.

The area leased to Great Britain as shown on the annexed map includes the waters of Mirs Bay and Deep Bay, but it is agreed that Chinese vessels of war, whether neutral or otherwise, shall retain the right to use those waters.

This Convention shall come into force on the first day of July, eighteen hundred and ninety-eight, being the thirteenth day of the fifth moon of the twenty fourth year of Kuang Hsü. It shall be ratified by the sovereigns of the two countries, and the ratifications shall be exchanged in London as soon as possible.

In witness whereof the undersigned, duly authorised thereto by their respective governments, have signed the present agreement. Done at Peking in quadruplicate (four copies in English and four in Chinese) the ninth day of June in the year of Our Lord eighteen hundred and ninety-eight, being the twenty first day of the fourth moon of the twenty fourth year of Kuang Hsü.

Claude M. MacDonald

The Thin Red Line

Dotted along the hills above the frontier with China is a series of toytown forts that look as if they belong on the set of a Beau Geste film. They're called Mackenzie Forts after the man who designed then. They sport battlements and parapets, and from their roofs fly large Union Jacks which seem out of scale with the little buildings beneath them. These are the posts from which the border is policed. Their significance is almost entirely psychological—wars aren't fought from forts nowadays. Manning each one is a small detachment of Hong Kong police and a few dozen Gurkha soldiers. A couple of years ago there were three or four battalions of soldiers guarding the twenty-six mile frontier—now there's only one and they are normally Gurkhas. As a result of their nocturnal work, most of them sleep during the day, and at times there are only 100 armed soldiers guarding Hong Kong during daylight.

Apart from one British battalion, which is posted here on rotation from home, the other four battalions of Hong Kong's garrison are Gurkhas. It seems strangely appropriate that the last frontier of empire should be guarded by the last vestiges of an imperial army. The Gurkhas are the only mercenary army in the classic sense still operating in the modern world.

Not that it will be much of a stand if the need to fight should arise. The garrison has no planes, no missiles, no artillery. No one expects to be able to defend Hong Kong against any determined attack from China. As one senior civil servant put it, 'I sometimes wonder why we bother—it'll just take one phone call from Peking and we'll all be on the boat home.' The garrison's main duties are chasing illegal immigrants and providing the occasional guard of honour, but the Gurkhas know that ultimately they are an indulgence—the last symbols of an option which does not exist. They are more likely to vanish as a result of a Whitehall defence cut than enemy action.

The Lease for the New Territories.

be rehoused out of the cramped squalor of Kowloon into the gleaming new cities that are springing up in the New Territories.

Three cities the size of Southampton and a clutch of smaller towns are being built at breakneck pace in the area covered by the lease. Massive tower blocks, huge reclamation projects, roads, tunnels, railways and the like are being carved out of the green landscape of the New Territories. Places like Tuen Mun and Sha Tin represent for Hong Kongers a glimpse of a better tomorrow—one they want to happen but can see vanishing if nothing is done about the legal position of the New Territories. Without them, Hong Kong cannot survive.

The New Territories are also Hong Kong's lung—the vital bit of fresh air that makes life in a crowded community tolerable. Hong Kong is one of the most crowded places on earth, with a population density in parts twenty times that of Britain, and it must have some space in which to breathe if it is to survive. Viewed from the air downtown Hong Kong and Kowloon are brown and grey smudges, unrelieved high-rise building. By contrast, fly over the hills of the New Territories and you see green fields, trees and jungle.

And it's not only housing or leisure opportunities that are being provided in the New Territories. Industry, short of space in the harbour area, is moving out to the new towns. Huge quantities of public capital are going into the area. New lines for the Mass Transit Railway (Hong Kong's equivalent of the underground) are being built out into the new towns of the north. Even the Jockey Club, most sacred of all institutions in Hong Kong, has established itself in the New Territories with a gleaming new racetrack at Sha Tin.

Government is by far the biggest spender in the New Territories. Patrick Hase, the man in charge of building the new city of Sha Tin, which will be home to three-quarters of a million Hong Kongers in about ten years' time, realises that he is building for the future—a future that will be here long after he has gone. 'It is a gesture of faith in the future. A town of this size, once built, will be here forever, whatever and whoever is the political structure on top of it. The town is being built with a view not to the next ten years, but to the next hundred or two hundred years.' It's an admirable if somewhat grandiloquent point of view, and one that a public servant dedicated to not rocking the boat could be expected to give.

For others, such as the private developers who are following government in investing in the cities of the New Territories, the problem is more immediate. Nearly half the money invested at Sha Tin will be private and it will be money looking for a return before the end of the lease. As that period decreases, the anxiety of investors increases. Developer David Chan, who was himself born in the New Territories and is now investing heavily there, is typical of many. Though his existing schemes are going ahead, he's stalling on future projects—including a massive leisure complex north of Yuen Long—until the future looks a bit clearer.

If within the next two years Britain and China do not actively discuss the lease problem, then I think that as a businessman in Hong Kong I

Sha Tin—once an inlet now a fast-growing city.

will find it very difficult to make decisions on my investment projects. If it's not discussed we'll lose the confidence to invest in Hong Kong.

But like many here, Chan is sceptical that Britain and China will do anything.

> In Britain you have your problems—unemployment, the economy, Northern Ireland—Hong Kong is low down on the agenda. The same in China—they have the modernisation of China's economy, Taiwan, lots of things to worry about. Hong Kong is about number 100 on their list.

One factor that might speed a solution would be the fear of people like David Chan losing the confidence to invest in Hong Kong. If there is any simple way of describing Hong Kong it is as a triumph of improbable confidence over harsh reality. Those whose businesses depend on confidence know the truth of that. The man who has transformed the skyline of Hong Kong Island over the last few years, Trevor Bedford, managing director of the colony's biggest property company, Hong Kong Land, is just one of the businessmen who are worried about the uncertainties of the future. Bedford is brutally frank. 'Hong Kong is about one thing and one thing only—confidence. When that confidence begins to wane it will begin to affect investment.' There are no signs of that—yet.

7

The biggest worry for those with a stake in the future of Hong Kong is that foreign investment—at the moment flooding in—will suddenly cut off. Foreign money is the lifeblood of the place. But the hands on the switches controlling the flow aren't in Hong Kong. They belong to businessmen in other countries who are influenced in their decisions by what the politicians in London or Peking say. Those who live in the colony know that whatever they do won't make much difference—Hong Kong's fate is not in Hong Kong's hands. At the moment neither London nor Peking seem much inclined to do anything about it. Partly it's because they've other priorities, pressing domestic problems that require urgent solutions; partly it is because they simply don't know what to do. This applies to both sides.

China does not recognise the lease, or indeed any of the treaties which ceded Chinese territory to Britain. It regards them as unequal, enforced on China by a strong imperialist power at a time when it was weak. Britain's attitude is scarcely more helpful. If the Chinese feel they have had a rough deal in the past, Britain's view is heavily tinged with guilt at being the instigator of that rough dealing. To some in Hong Kong, this sense of guilt is standing in the way of settlement. It produces fears of a sell-out. Some Hong Kongers suspect that Britain regards the place as a tiresome relic of a bygone colonial age, to be discarded as soon as possible.

The Foreign Office, of course, denies any such feelings and maintains that it is anxious to seek a just and lasting settlement of the Hong Kong problem. Not unreasonably they claim the ball is firmly in Peking's court, and that they are willing to enter into negotiations on the future of Hong Kong at any time—negotiations that they hope will ensure the continuation of Hong Kong's strange position. The most recent British minister to discuss the question with the Chinese, Humphrey Atkins, who resigned as Lord Privy Seal over the Falkland Islands affair, felt he detected a tiny movement in China's views on the subject: 'I found the Chinese government recognised the fact that this is not a problem that can be left to the last possible moment. But they aren't ready to make any definite proposals or engage in substantive discussions at the moment.'

Atkins describes the current position in language so obscure that one realises why it is that Foreign Office men are called Mandarins: 'They haven't yet decided their posture but they are going to address themselves to it.' That is the Foreign Office way of saying the Chinese haven't a clear idea of what to do about Hong Kong. They are thinking about thinking about it.

The next move is clearly for the Chinese to make, but there are many in Hong Kong who recognise the vital role that Britain must play and who fear that she may tire of the whole exercise and offload the colony onto China. So the leaders of the community have devised an ingenious set of incentives aimed at keeping the British public—and government—from feeling that Hong Kong is a burden.

The incentives are massive—big contracts for British industry designed to remind the British that having an empire can be valuable. There is the Castle Peak Power station (see p. 10) which represents Britain's largest ever export order and should keep thousands of British workers in jobs for a decade or so. There is also the Mass Transit Railway where Britain managed to get the contract for design, engineering and rolling stock after a Japanese consortium stated it would be unable to fulfill the contract. The Kowloon–Canton railway is being re-equipped with rolling stock made by Metro Cammell in Birmingham; the same company is supplying hundreds of buses to Hong Kong. These contracts are worth thousands of millions of pounds and mean thousands of jobs—a formidable bribe to maintain Britain's interest in Hong Kong. And to make doubly sure, Hong Kong arranges things so that running the colony costs Britain nothing. For example it pays for its own defence: three-quarters of the estimated £120m cost of Hong Kong's defence is born by the colony's taxpayers.

In one respect the British connection is vitally important and cannot be disregarded. However much Britain might wish otherwise, Hong Kong is, politically speaking, a legal fiction enacted by the British Parliament. One option that isn't open to Hong Kong or Britain is to ignore that fact, go our respective ways and forget about 1997. As Jimmy MacGregor of the Hong Kong Chamber of Commerce pointed out, 'We can't just go up and past 1997 with a nudge and a wink. It requires positive action.' According to British law, no action of the British or Hong Kong governments can have legal force after 30 June 1997 in the New Territories. No policeman could arrest anyone. Even now all leases on land in the New Territories end three days before the theoretical end of British rule there—presumably so that the landlord, the government of Hong Kong, can organise a good springclean before handing the whole place back to China.

Seen from the British end of the telescope, the idea that Britain might be willing, yet again, to cut and run from a tiresome commitment, doesn't seem implausible. There is no doubt that since the last war, Britain has become a very insular place. The strength of reaction against membership of the Common Market shows that. Many in Hong Kong see it as their role to lift British eyes from butter mountains and wine lakes to look again at the big world outside. Hong Kong has inherited none of Britain's introspection.

One of the strongest impressions a visitor gets of Hong Kong is the degree to which the colony looks outwards. Put simply, it has to. Looking inwards all you see is one huge, overcrowded and noisy building site so looking outwards to the rest of the world is essential. There's plenty to see, for Hong Kong is becoming the focus of the fastest growing part of the world—the dynamic economies of South East Asia. Japan, Korea, Taiwan, Singapore, Hong Kong—these are all places growing at a phenomenal rate, much faster than Europe and America.

Dr Gordon Redding of Hong Kong University sees this area as the future centre of the world economy.

We are seeing at the moment an economic miracle based on the Confucian type cultures of South East Asia plus the Japanese. Over the next one hundred years the miracle is going to overtake Britain. And here is Britain with a chance to be right bang in the middle of it, as a key element in it.

The Power Game

Perched on the corner of a mountain on the western side of the New Territories stands a symbol of Hong Kong's confidence in itself and its future. It's a power station—and on a scale which takes the breath away. Castle Peak is a massive project—the type of undertaking that even Britain would think twice about. Here though, it is going ahead, backed by private capital. Already it's an impressive sight—a big hole in the ground out of which is rising an edifice larger than St Paul's Cathedral, which is in turn dwarfed by a monstrous concrete chimney.

When finished it will be the largest power station in Asia. It's the biggest of the incentives Hong Kong is offering Britain to take an interest in what happens to the colony. Nearly all of its equipment is British—turbines from General Electric Company, miles of cabling from Associated Electrical Industries, cranes from Clarke Chapman, orders which collectively add up to well over £600m and make it the largest ever single export order for Britain.

Of course it'll take some time to complete—indeed the finance package which is paying for it runs through to the year 2002, five years after the end of the lease on the land upon which it stands. But the owners of the venture, the Hong Kong-based China Light and Power and the American oil company Exxon, are not worried about such technicalities. They've taken out insurance. The station will burn a lot of Chinese coal and in return, about 10 per cent of its power output will go back to China. As a symbol of their good faith, the pylons that will link Castle Peak to China have already been built. Exxon has another reason for the investment. They are keen to have a slice of the offshore oil exploration work that China is soon going to be handing out. Since China is expected to have reserves—on and offshore—comparable to those of Saudi Arabia, that would be a prize well worth the risk. Exxon hopes that backing Castle Peak will help its chances of taking part.

Exxon denies that the two are related—as its manager in Hong Kong put it, 'We regard both these projects as discrete investments, not related to each other.' However, in a venture like this with huge sums at risk, many believe that you don't gamble $6 billion US—Exxon's stake in Castle Peak—without aiming to land a big prize at the end of the game.

Pigs in transit from China across the border, bound for the slaughterhouse.

Others, like Michael Sandberg, chairman of the Hong Kong and Shanghai Bank, are convinced that Britain must raise its eyes from contemplation of its immediate problems and see what Hong Kong has to offer. It's a change of perspective that he feels is beginning to happen:

> I think very much in the last ten or twelve years the cry has been, go East young man, rather than go West. A lot of people don't seem to appreciate what a large modern city this is. They still come out expecting to see James Bond chasing Fu Manchu down the street.

But such pleas that Hong Kong be taken seriously are significant not so much for the response—which is slight in Britain— as for the fact that they are made in the first place. Hong Kong feels distinctly unloved in, and unwanted by, Britain. To counter that it has decided to make itself useful to the other party in this curious triangle—Peking. Hong Kong knows that without Peking it cannot survive in the long term. Or even in the short term.

Just next to the Man Kam To road bridge into China is a modest little building which emits a high-pitched whirring. It's the power source which keeps Hong Kong's life-support system going. Hong Kong is short of the most basic resource in the world—water. With little land and a bulging population the colony has to import about half its water from China. The pipeline is the most important single fact of Hong Kong's political economy.

To help pay for the water and the other products it buys from China—nearly all its food, for example, comes across the border—and to secure its future, Hong Kong has to make itself as valuable to China as possible. It does so by acting as a sort of two-way translator—interpreting China to the world and, equally important, the world to China. In the days when China was a forbidden country, one of Hong Kong's biggest growth industries was China-watching on behalf of everyone else. Expert Peking watchers sprouted from every hillside, or more frequently every bar, interpreting Peking's every move to an uncomprehending world.

Now that tourists can come and go freely round most of China, that role has vanished. But another has been created. As China opens its doors to the West again, Hong Kong has become a vital part of the process, explaining China's requirements to the hordes of Western businessmen keen to gain a slice of the world's largest unexploited market. And as China has looked outwards again, it has found it needs Hong Kong to explain the ways of the inscrutable West.

In this new role, Hong Kong hopes it has found the insurance policy that will eventually make possible a settlement to the looming problem of 1997 and the lease. One businessman in Hong Kong summed up their attitude: 'If we make ourselves useful to China they won't think of doing away with Hong Kong.'

Or will they? The fundamental divergence between a free-booting capitalist economy dedicated to the free market and a centralised state-controlled communist economy must lead to tensions. No amount of wishful thinking—of which there is much in Hong Kong—can remove that reality. Even if the economies of communism and capitalism can live side by side, history cannot be rewritten or forgotten. Politics do not go away that easily.

CHAPTER TWO
LIVING IN A HURRICANE

In Britain, any businessman faced with Hong Kong's uncertain future would hesitate before investing. Paying off industrial loans, getting your money back over fifteen years would be a risky undertaking, not to be entered into lightly. In Hong Kong if you haven't made your money back more quickly than that—and several times over—you shouldn't be in business. The view is that Chinese policy may or may not change, that the lease may be renewed or it may not be. Either way the only thing to do is to get on with the business of making money now. It's an attitude which helps create an exciting and exhausting pace of life. Living for the present is an integral part of Hong Kong's lifestyle. In the time left before the lease runs out several fortunes can be made and lost at Hong Kong pace. One suspects that even if the problem of the lease did not exist the Chinese community of Hong Kong would still live that same way—it's the only life they know.

The sense of living on the edge of a volcano, of acting as if each moment might be your last, is central to Hong Kong. It's a view that has its roots deep in the insecurity of a people who have been refugees most of their lives. Dr Gordon Redding of Hong Kong University is one Westerner who has studied this phenomenon. He sees Hong Kongers as a people on the run, rootless refugees who must make the best of every opportunity that presents itself: 'They're used to being pushed around, it has been part of the lifestyle of the overseas Chinese for centuries. They have to take a fairly short term, pragmatic as they say, view of what life is all about.' Pragmatism is a word the visitor encounters continually in Hong Kong. It means making the best of whatever circumstances you find yourself in, being able to turn potential disaster into realisable profit and, most important of all, doing it quickly before someone else gets there first. It makes for a fast-moving community. As Dr Redding says, 'It's reflected in their business behaviour, in pay-back periods of three or four years, as opposed to a much longer term repayment period in the West.' He sees that as an enormous strength: 'It uses capital much more effectively, it makes them fast on their feet. There's a kind of hunger drive here, a powerful need, and as long as they are short of money they will work hard.'

The refugee part of Hong Kong's population knows what being poor is all about. The upheavals of twentieth-century China—the Second World War and the civil war that followed it—persuaded or forced millions of mainland Chinese to seek a better life elsewhere. They travelled to Taiwan,

A Day at the Races

In the traditional Chinese view of life there are four vices: women, gambling, drinking and smoking—in that order. Hong Kong caters extensively to all of them, particularly the second. Gambling as such is banned in Hong Kong; it is illegal to put money on a game of Mah Jong, though many do. The only official outlet for the Chinese passion for gambling is horse racing; and that is tremendously popular. There are sixty-five race meetings a year—each one draws a crowd of between 30,000 and 40,000 people. Those who can't go to the track bet off course. The Jockey Club, which controls all racing and betting—on or off course—estimates that 500,000 people bet each week on the races—almost one in ten of the population. The amounts gambled are stupendous; last year betting turnover was almost £1 billion sterling, not far short of the figure in Britain. On one day, I saw the gross betting take for the previous night's racing at Happy Valley brought in to the bank—seven black boxes containing well over £2 million, almost the equivalent of the Great Train Robbery. Most betting is not on a simple win or place—though you can make such bets—it's a much more complicated system involving combinations of placings in the same or different races. They're called quinellas. Thus you can bet on one horse coming third in a race and another fourth. If either horse fails to gain its place, you lose. If both bets are right the long odds ensure a big payout for a small stake. It appeals to the Chinese fondness for taking a wild risk in their gambling. The Chinese gambler dislikes safe bets; he would rather take frequent small losses in the hope of one day hitting the jackpot. Odds of 70 and 80 to 1 are normal in quenella bets.

Hong Kong may not approve of gambling, but it is willing to profit from it. After the costs of race administration have been met, the government takes its cut in the form of a tax. The rest is distributed to various charities. In 1981 £25 million was donated to a wide range of charities. Five hundred pounds was given to the Norwegian Missionary Society, £3 million to a new sports centre. Over the years since the scheme started it has given away well over £50 million. It's a typical example of Hong Kong's pragmatism—if you can't eliminate an anti-social activity, make sure that the profit from it goes to benefit the community at large. Gambling thus becomes not a vice but a virtuous act of charity. That's called killing two birds with one stone.

Singapore, Malaya, the United States—anywhere, in fact, that would take them in and give them the security so lacking at home. Hong Kong took more than its fair share of these people escaping from chaos. In 1945 Hong Kong's population was less than half a million—today it's about five and a half million, half of them refugees from China. In the last five years alone half a million people have crossed, legally and illegally, from China. The rule in Hong Kong has been that these new arrivals start at the bottom of the pile.

The hunger drive to get out from the bottom of that pile has turned the countries of South East Asia where they settled into the fastest growing economies in the world. Two places in particular have benefited— Singapore and Hong Kong. Both are Chinese-dominated societies, small city states that have carved a niche for themselves in the world's industrial and financial markets. The success they've achieved shows what can be done, given a starting point where you have nothing and only the determination to get something. Singapore's Prime Minister, Lee Kwan Yu, has tried to ensure that in the process of pulling themselves up by their bootstraps, his people do not forget where they came from. He's coined the phrase 'the rugged society'—meaning that Singapore must stay rugged if it is to stay successful. In Hong Kong no one needs to coin such a phrase—it's a fact of life. Responding to the challenge of the new is a vital motivating force.

In Britain the Industrial Revolution took place over almost a century. Steady change gradually transformed an agricultural society into an industrial one. In Hong Kong it has happened almost overnight; within a couple of decades peasant farmers from China have been turned into industrial workers. Today Hong Kong is among the top ten of the world's industrial nations, and is aiming to become the third financial centre in the world after New York and London. The hunger drive still works.

The rewards have been tangible too. Real wages are rising fast and the standard of living is now second only to the major economies of Europe, North America and Japan. And Hong Kong is closing the gap. According to one government official, at the current rate, Hong Kong's wealth per head could pass Britain's in a decade. In Hong Kong one is surrounded by the visible results of that success story. As far as Hong Kongers are concerned, the point about making money is showing it. The place is a monument to conspicuous, even vulgar consumption.

One night I dined with a group of young Chinese businessmen in their thirties—a lawyer, an accountant and a couple of property developers. They spoke Cantonese for most of the meal, occasionally interpreting an outline of the conversation for me. At one stage the conversation between them became a heated argument. After listening for a few minutes I asked what they were arguing about. One of them had decided that his new Mercedes should be a vivid shade of green and the other three, who were also buying new Mercedes, were trying to persuade him that this was a bit over the top.

One product that you don't really have to push in Hong Kong is the Mercedes car. It is the vital symbol of success and there are more of them per head of the population than anywhere else in the world. Indeed I calculated

The jumbo floating restaurant in Aberdeen Harbour.

that if all the Mercedes in Hong Kong came onto the colony's roads at the same time, they alone would take up one-eighth of the road surface. Mercedes and Rolls Royces aren't in what salesmen call a 'price sensitive market'. Despite the fact that a Mercedes costs about twice what it would in Europe, demand shows no signs of slackening. There are other luxury products which sell equally well, but few are as visible a sign of having made it as a Merc. To add the final gloss, the successful businessman will try and get a car number plate with as many 8's in it as possible. The word for eight in Cantonese sounds like the word for prosperity, so the prudent—or should it be superstitious—businessman who wants to ensure the continued prosperity of his business will buy the right number plate. One Rolls Royce in Hong Kong has four eights in the number plate, and reputedly last changed hands—the plate that is, not the car—for £25,000 two years ago. Gordon Redding again: 'Money is a religion in this part of the world—and understandably so because there is very little else upon which to base life's values. This is a very insecure place.'

In Chinese the notion of being prosperous can be expressed as 'having a full rice bowl'. It's a neat symbol of what most of the refugees who came here were looking for. Though the Hong Kong of today is a long way from starving, the notion that the rice bowl could ever be empty again haunts people. Psychologists claim that insecure people are heavy eaters—and observation of Hong Kong seems to bear that out.

One of the great institutions of Hong Kong is eating out. Devouring the full rice bowl ostentatiously and, it must be said, noisily in public is an essential part of the Hong Kong way of life. Nowhere on earth has as many restaurants as Hong Kong. Whereas for the Westerner eating out is an occasional luxury to be enjoyed once or twice a week, in Hong Kong it's a daily ritual of great significance. In part that's for strictly practical reasons. Living in crowded conditions in a city that has expanded too fast for its own good means that to make life tolerable the family must be able to get out of the house. Cooking, eating, sleeping and doing homework all in one room imposes heavy strains on everyone, not least the person doing the cooking. Hong Kong caters massively to the desire to eat out. It boasts the largest restaurant in the world in Kowloon which seats 6,500 people at a sitting.

The ritual of eating out is also a symbol that for the moment, it's possible to relax and enjoy the fruits of success. For a generation that knows what starvation means, that is an achievement. For the visitor though, it has a side which is less appealing. The Chinese business banquet is a major undertaking, requiring careful pacing to get through the mountains of food involved. Fourteen or fifteen courses are not uncommon, washed down with endless cups of Chinese tea, and many meals go on for hours as rare delicacies arrive one after another. Contrary to popular myth one does not see dog on the menu. Hong Kongers are too Westernised and aware of our susceptibilities for that. Their cousins in China, however, think differently. I know of one businesswoman who is running out of excuses for not eating dog on her frequent trips to China. She has to explain shamefacedly to her puzzled hosts that it's the product of her Western upbringing. Dogs are for walking not eating. It is a point of view the Chinese find difficult to understand; dog is a great delicacy in a society that is short of meat.

To mainland Chinese the refusal to include dog on the menu is merely a product of Hong Kong's contamination by Western customs. More seriously they regard the people of Hong Kong with some suspicion precisely because they have lost much of their Chineseness. Hong Kongers are now far removed from traditional Chinese ethics and behaviour. It is clearly un-Chinese not only to be successful but then to enjoy telling everyone about it. But it is this subtly blended cocktail of East and West that is Hong Kong's unique quality. Both British and Chinese seem to have drawn something from each other. The British are content to provide the structure within which Hong Kong operates—a legal system, a currency, a form of government; while the Chinese provide a flexibility and adaptability to changing circumstances that keeps the place quick on its feet. Just as Westerners need the entrepreneurial talent of the Chinese, so the Chinese need the framework of Western law to provide stability and direction. The result is a magical combination.

Hong Kong's economic growth is only now beginning to respond to the downturn in world trade. As recently as 1981 the growth rate was running at more than 10 per cent per annum. Currently it has slowed down, but it will probably pick up again as the world emerges from recession. The fact that Hong Kong hasn't suffered more has much to do with the unique environment that this Sino-British combination encourages.

Some years ago the government decided it should do something to

A rare sight in Hong Kong—a street beggar.

promote small businesses. It set up a government-supported loan scheme to help small companies finance themselves. The scheme was wound up in 1976—because of lack of demand. Not that there weren't the small businesses; on the contrary Hong Kong's economy relies on the small business. The scheme failed because the Chinese entrepreneur believes in self-help. A new business is financed from hard-earned savings and, if available, money from members of the family. The last place the Hong Konger would look for money would be the government—to do so would involve an immense loss of face. It would be a defeat for the principle of self-reliance.

Small businesses flourish in Hong Kong. There are more than 45,000 businesses in the territory. Using the British definition of a small business— one employing less than 200 people—99 per cent of Hong Kong's businesses are small. The average number of employees per business is only twenty. Part of the reason for this lies in the psychology of the Chinese. Why be an employee when you can be your own boss? A typical example of the type is the personal assistant to the chairman of one of Hong Kong's biggest Chinese banks. He's been in the job for a couple of years and has used the opportunity to learn all he can about banking. He's not interested in a boardroom job at his boss's bank—which he could certainly get—he's going to set up in business on his own.

The other reason for this flourishing of small businesses is the geography of the place. There simply isn't room for the large-scale heavy manufacturing industries that dominate the economies of Europe and North America. With limited land and no natural resources, Hong Kong has to make up in skill and speed for what it lacks in resources and size. There is no heavy engineering, no large-scale shipbuilding, no big steel plants, no motor industry—all those goods are imported. Instead Hong Kong has had to concentrate on industries which require small premises, little start-up capital and simple machinery. That too has its advantages. If you have only a small amount of capital tied up in a business you can afford to switch production from one product to another very swiftly. You also do not have to worry about the problems of decline inevitably associated with heavy industries.

Conic Electronics is a good example. It's an unknown name in the West but its products are well known—many of the electronics sold in Western high-street shops under their own brand names come from Conic's factories in Hong Kong. Founded in 1965, its real growth started in distinctly upromising circumstances, during the upheavals of 1967. In that year the Red Guards were on the rampage in China where the Cultural Revolution was at its height and there were regular confrontations between troops and rioters on the streets of Hong Kong. Many businessmen were worried and started to sell up. The founder of Conic, Alex Au, bought some plastic moulding machinery cheap and expanded his business. It was a shrewd gamble—Hong Kong calmed down and life returned to normal. Conic was making the plastic bodies for various electronics goods, but Mr Au decided that the future was in the electronics inside his plastics. He moved into calculators, TV sets, watches, electronic toys—anything, in fact, which made use of the silicon chip. His latest boom product is the telephone-answering machine in the wake of the British government's decision to legalise the sale of such machines in the UK. A market has been created overnight for a new product.

The production lines in Mr Au's factories are odd to the Western eye—there are many more work benches than there are people. Each row of benches represents a product line, and the flexibility of Conic is such that labour can be switched easily from TV sets to calculators or to whatever product is in demand. Mr Au is keeping Conic one step ahead of the game by investing heavily in automated machinery. Hong Kong wage rates, he complains, are now approaching £10 a day which means his products will soon cease to be competitive with those of the cheaper countries in Asia. His response has been to automate—it lowers costs and ensures greater reliability. Reacting to the demands of the marketplace and your competitors is vital to the success of a business like Mr Au's. He has now got the reward for being an entrepreneur. Recently when Conic went public and issued shares, they were snapped up by the market. The company was valued at over £35 million. Few British companies could have come to that from nowhere in fifteen years.

An important part of the success of companies like Conic has been sheer hard work. It's a part of the Hong Kong philosophy that anyone doing business here has to accept. During dinner with the manager of one British company, he excused himself from the dinner table at 10.30 p.m., explain-

ing that he had to get back to work. He had arrived in the office at 8 a.m. and had not left until after 7 p.m., and he was now returning to report to his London office as it opened on the business done during the day in Hong Kong. He does this six days a week, but he'd chosen the job and was making a lot of money doing it—well over £30,000 per annum, with accommodation paid for and tax at 15 per cent. In three years he would return to the UK, a wealthy man.

The central district of Hong Kong from the peak.

For the Westerner accustomed to a more relaxed attitude to a job Hong Kong is a little frightening. The place really does believe in the virtues of hard work. According to government statistics over half the working population works more than fifty hours a week. Having two or more jobs is not unusual. One expatriate summed the atmosphere up thus:

> You get out exactly what you put in. I felt that in the UK I probably wasn't getting out what I was putting in. In Britain you can work very hard and not exactly get much more for it in job satisfaction, salary, whatever. You can work not very hard and probably still earn the same as someone who does work hard. Here it is quite a bit different, the harder you work, the more you put into it, the more you jolly well get out of it.

Such an urge to acquire wealth would be regarded as extreme elsewhere—in Hong Kong your material success is the measure of your worth. The expatriate community—mainly British, American and Australian—has adapted to the ruthlessly materialistic lifestyle of Hong Kong. It's a lifestyle which leaves little room for activities of an unprofitable nature. Few people have much leisure. Indeed if they had it, they wouldn't know what to do with it. Apart from limited sports facilities, Hong Kong is desperately short of recreational possibilities or the space to put them in. Culturally it's a desert—with few theatres, playing host to the occasional visiting company, a handful of cinemas (mostly showing Bruce Lee films), and a few British Council lectures or visiting Chinese dance groups. Not much for a city of five and a half million.

On the other hand Hong Kong has too much of other amenities. It is probably the most over-banked place in the world. While in Britain there is approximately one bank account for every two of the population, in Hong Kong there's more than one per head. Since not many children have accounts, this means that many adults have two or more. And there are banks on every street corner. The Chinese are highly sophisticated about money and would not think of leaving it under the mattress. If you visit the Queen's Road Central branch of the Hong Kong and Shanghai Bank you'll see that sophistication in action. It boasts the highest turnover of money of any single retail banking outlet in the world. There's row after row of tellers, and long queues as customers move money from account to account, buy and sell gold, and engage in every conceivable form of financial transaction. They'll move their money from one account to another in the lunchbreak to take advantage of a tiny change in interest rates. Money sitting still is money wasting away.

The result is a system that competes vigorously for business, to the benefit of the customer. In the staid world of British banking, the cosy relationship of the big four high-street banks ensures that competition is limited, and efficiency is low. By contrast, to open an account in Hong Kong takes about fifteen minutes. The bank, on this particular occasion, was most apologetic that it could not provide a cheque book and cheque card until two hours later—the printer had gone out to lunch. No British bank could match that. One of the pleasant consequences of so much competition in the marketplace is that the consumer tends to get a better deal than elsewhere. The attitude that service is a luxury has no place in Hong Kong. If one shop won't meet your demands and your price, it's too easy to walk down the street to another.

The attitude permeates even the area that is normally most uncompetitive, the public telephone monopoly. The Hong Kong phone system not only works but also copes with demand. It is owned by a private company —it is a licensed monopoly with its rate of profit controlled by government. In return for the monopoly it is required to deliver what the customer wants. To have a telephone installed takes 24 hours if you're lucky or a good customer, like a bank, and is guaranteed within a few days. Local calls, that is to say calls made inside the boundaries of Hong Kong, are free—included in the rental of £10 a quarter—and the system is modern—it's had computerised directory inquiries for almost five years. It is even possible to get a phone for that smallest of small businesses—a street barrow. A barrow selling lampshades near the Hilton Hotel has its own phone.

It's a business attitude which owes more to the United States than to the regulated economies of Western Europe—the attitude that what the customers want is what you ought to be giving them. For underlying the dedication to hard work and the sheer competitive efficiency of Hong Kong is an economic philosophy which ensures that the weak go to the wall and the strong survive.

Hong Kong is probably the last place on earth that practises free-market economics, thereby earning much praise from the world's leading monetarist, Milton Friedman. Classic laissez-faire economics—Adam Smith's philosophy that the marketplace should be allowed to rule—has survived in Hong Kong long after it has been abandoned elsewhere. The central tenet of laissez-faire, that government should stand remote from the operations of the market, is maintained. The government's economic policy is described by a curious phrase that sounds self-contradictory—'positive non-intervention'. 'It's a government appreciation that a banker probably knows more about banking than a civil servant', explains Hong Kong and Shanghai Bank chairman, Michael Sandberg, 'and that a shirt maker knows more about shirt making than a civil servant. A man should stick to his last, government should stick to governing, bankers to banking, and shirt makers to making shirts.' In practice this means that government does not interfere, as it would in Britain or the United States, to stop failures going to the wall. If Chrysler had been a Hong Kong company, it would have gone down and that would have been that. The government's view would have been that if the marketplace could not sustain a demand for Chrysler's products at a price that was profitable then Chrysler should stop making them. It is the market which must decide how to redeploy the assets invested in Chrysler—not government.

Conveniently, this laissez-faire attitude accords well with the refugee psychology of Hong Kong. It echoes the cry of the Chinese business community: set the rules and leave us be. The tax regime surrounding business is easy-going and generous, with income tax at 15 per cent, corporation tax at 16½ per cent, no capital gains tax and no foreign exchange control. Government officials see it as the only possible course of action for an economy with no natural resources and no international political clout. As Bill Dorward, Director of Trade, points out:

> We really don't have anything except people and entrepreneurial skill. We have that in abundance. To live in a competitive world means your traders and your industrialists have got to be tough, active and imaginative and your workforce has got to have a dedication and a work ethic which regrettably has been lost in many countries.

This urge to self-help, the entrepreneurial skill that Bill Dorward is so keen to leave to flourish, is practised on every street corner in Hong Kong. The colony is alive with street traders and hawkers—so much so that periodic though unsuccessful attempts are made by government to limit their numbers. In the 1976 census more than 50,000 people listed their occupa-

The Crocodile

Making a fast buck is almost a constitutional right in Hong Kong and many have grown rich out of catering to the desire for sudden riches. Go to the first floor of the Admiralty Tower, one of the biggest sky-scrapers in central Hong Kong, and you will be ushered into the offices of Sun Hung Kai Securities. If you say you're interested in buying some shares, they'll direct you to their public dealing room, known more colloquially in Hong Kong as the 'Goldfish Bowl'. The name refers to the rows of television screens along one wall which enable punters to keep up with the latest prices via a video link to the Stock Exchange. On the other side of the room is a bank of telephones and data terminals—manned by Sun Hung Kai staff—through which you can place your bets. If it sounds a bit like a branch of Ladbroke's, it looks just like that too. People walk in off the streets, bearing sandwiches and flasks of Chinese tea, and settle in for a day's flutter. Anyone can play, and the volatility of the market is such that you can win—or lose—large sums of money very easily. It's a scene you wouldn't find anywhere else in the world, where stock exchanges are seen as forbidding places, dominated by professionals and inaccess-ible to the man in the street. Inventing the 'Goldfish Bowl' has made the chairman of Sun Hung Kai a very rich man. Fung King Hey is a very successful businessman, known only half-jokingly in Hong Kong as 'The Crocodile'—a winner in the city's tough world of business. He started his stockbroking company in 1969 with a staff of seven. Today he's expanded into banking and financial services and has more than a thousand employees, and total assets of more than half a billion sterling. The company is dedicated to a very simple principle—returning profits which outpace Hong Kong's own econo-mic growth. A formidable target but one it is meeting comfortably. The company is now opening offices across Europe and North America. Fung is still loyal to the clients who started him in busi-ness—taxi drivers, amahs (household servants), factory workers. The majority of the portfolios he manages involve less than £1,000 worth of investments, but, as Mr Fung says, 'Collectively they make up a formidable force on the Hong Kong stock market.' One estimate has it that one-quarter of Hong Kong's daily market turnover goes through the offices of Sun Hung Kai.

tion as hawking. In times of recession the numbers rise. It is not, however, regarded as a shameful activity or any sign of failure to get a proper job if you take to hawking. In true Hong Kong style, hawking is regarded as a small business. Try telling the shoe shine man outside the Mandarin Hotel that he's any different from the shipping millionaire whose shoes he cleans. He'll tell you it's just a matter of scale.

The modern gambling den—watching stock exchange trading on TV.

As long as the boom continues, no one questions the economic philosophy or the ethics behind it. John Bremridge, the Financial Secretary to the Hong Kong government and the man responsible for the colony's economic policy, is refreshingly honest about the government's reluctance to plan ahead:

> I hate looking ahead. You can talk about looking ahead ten or fifteen years—in this part of the world five years is a lifetime. All I can really hope to do is to set up a state of affairs in which people are pretty nimble on their feet. You get very rigid if you start thinking in terms of what's going to happen in ten or fifteen years. I don't know what's going to happen in two years.

CHAPTER THREE

THE BARREN ISLAND

Hong Kongers live for the present. They have little conception of what the future might hold and, as far as they're concerned, the past is dead and buried, ancient history to be forgotten. But Hong Kong is a classic example of a place whose future prospects can only be comprehended by studying the past; and its past is murky, for Hong Kong only came into existence as the by-product of a sordid nineteenth-century squabble over drug smuggling.

If today Hong Kong boasts of being a successful marriage of East and West, it is one of the few positive results of the meeting of the two cultures. The origins of Hong Kong were less auspicious, firmly rooted in a history of mutual incomprehension, aggression and distrust between China and Britain.

In 1848 the Chinese mandarin, Xu Ji Yu, in his *Manual of World Geography*, the first book to be written in China about Westerners, attempted to describe to his fellow countrymen the nation which had just humiliated them in war. He explained the British desire for trade with China thus: 'England consists merely of three islands, a handful of stones in the Western ocean. Her area is estimated to be about the same as Taiwan and Hainan. Even if the soil is all fertile, how much can be produced locally?' He went on to describe North America as a place, 'hanging isolated on the globe. Since ancient times it has been little known.' To understand why such an explanation was necessary is to understand much of the confused relationship between China and the West. In 1840 China was, in terms of land area and population, the largest country in the world. The ideological beliefs of China sustained the view that she was also the most powerful, civilised and significant country in the world. The Chinese believed that the world was square and the heaven above it was round. Heaven projected down onto earth a circular shadow. At the centre of that shadow lay China, whose name means the 'area beneath heaven'. Outside this area in the four corners of the square world, beyond the shadow of heaven, dwelt foreign barbarians, evil spirits and sea monsters. It followed that the notion of barbarians being people one could deal with on equal terms was absurd. 'The barbarians are like beasts, and not to be ruled by the same principles as the Chinese. Were one to attempt to control them by the great maxims of reason it would tend to nothing but the greatest confusion,' explained one writer. However, that did not stop the Chinese being polite (and somewhat patronising) to foreigners. The Chinese mandarin in charge of Canton, writing to Queen Victoria in 1839, stated kindly:

> Your country lies 20,000 leagues away; but for all that the way of heaven holds good for you as for us . . . Our Heavenly Court [the Emperor] treats all within the four seas as one great family . . . there is no region so wild or so remote that he does not cherish and tend it.

A further obstacle to good relations was the fact that most of the foreigners China was forced into contact with were traders. In the order of Confucian society, traders came fourth after scholars, peasants and artisans. Although by the nineteenth century China was rapidly becoming a nation of traders, traditional philosophy excluded them from reasonable consideration. In exasperation, the Viceroy of Canton explained this to Chinese merchants in 1834: 'The Emperor of Heaven appoints officials, civil to rule the people, military to control the wicked. But the petty affairs of commerce are to be directed by the merchants themselves. With such matters officials are not to be concerned.' This determined the attitude of officialdom to foreign, as well as Chinese, traders.

From earliest times Chinese official policy had been to keep contact with foreigners to a minimum. The first traders to enter China—Arabs and Persians in the twelfth century—were confined to a small area of Canton. They were instructed to run their own affairs with as little interference from, and inconvenience to, Chinese officialdom as possible. China did not want to know about foreigners or their merchandise. The first-ever communication from the Chinese court to a British sovereign, in the latter years of George III's reign, stated, 'There is nothing we lack, and we set no value on strange or ingenious objects . . . and have no use for your country's manufacturers.' It was not only a point of view based on arrogance but also a statement of fact. Provided China could feed itself, it did not need foreign goods to survive. It was economically self-sufficient, and, in the early years of foreign contact, many of its technological achievements were considerably in advance of the West. Unfortunately while the West profited from and developed Chinese and other inventions in a dynamic society, China stagnated, reluctant to apply the lessons of the innovations it had pioneered. China remained a closed society.

Nor was the prejudice all one-sided. While China refused to acknowledge the growing power and sophistication of Europe, Europe was in turn abysmally ignorant of China and Chinese customs. The legacy of ill-will between East and West was fuelled by the equally strong Western conviction that the Chinese were barbaric and unreasonable. Lord Elgin, one of the numerous British officials who attempted to negotiate terms for trade with China, announced with exasperation: 'The Chinese yield nothing to reason and everything to fear.'

The first Europeans to arrive off the Chinese coast in any number were traders, and it was they who were to determine the shape of relations between China and the West. While China wanted nothing from the West, the West knew that it wanted the products of China—spices, silk and later tea. It was the Portuguese who first discovered and made use of a direct sea route to China and their ships reached Canton in 1514. Twenty years before, an attempt to reach the spice areas of the East by sailing west had resulted in Columbus reaching the Americas. For the next hundred years the Portuguese were to dominate trade with China, but by the end of the sixteenth century the Dutch had entered the arena. Their prices were considered too high and a group of British traders decided to set up in competition. In 1600 the East India Company was founded and the first of its vessels to sail eastwards represented Britain's initial diplomatic contact with China. It was symbolic that the message to the Emperor from Queen Elizabeth should be written in Latin, the Western language of diplomacy, but one that was completely unknown in China. China ignored these new intruders.

It was not until 1715 that the East India Company established its first permanent base in China with a factory at Canton. These were not factories in the contemporary sense of manufacturing centres but trading bases operated by 'factors', merchants whose job was to oversee and manage operations. The Chinese, who had been persuaded against their better judgement to open some of their ports to trade in the late seventeenth century, made attempts in the mid-eighteenth century to confine foreign trade to Canton. They worked out a system whereby the impact of undesirable contact with the West could be kept to a minimum. Westerners were forced to deal exclusively with a group of Chinese merchants called 'officially authorised merchants'. They were known in Chinese as the Cohong, and had the duty of fixing prices and regulating the volume of trade. In return for the enormous profits this gave them, they were also held responsible for the behaviour of Western traders. Officials meanwhile issued regulations forbidding Chinese subjects from emigrating or travelling on foreign ships, and as the activities of Christian missionaries became more noticeable, Chinese were forbidden to become Christians. Most significant of all, it was made a serious crime to teach any foreigner the Chinese language.

Despite these measures the volume of trade increased, mainly because the British discovered the joys of tea drinking. Tea had been the universal beverage of the Chinese since the sixth century, and Chinese poets had sung its praises in ways that modern advertising might envy but would not dare to emulate: 'Tea tempers the spirits, harmonises the mind, dispels lassitude, and relieves fatigue; awakens thought and prevents drowsiness, lightens and refreshes the body and clears the perceptive faculties.' The first two canisters of China tea arrived in Britain in 1669, and by the end of the eighteenth century tea imports from China had reached 20,000,000 lb a year. So important had tea become to Britain's foreign trade that by the turn of the nineteenth century duties on tea made up about one-tenth of the British government's revenues. Government therefore had a vested interest in the continuance of trade with China; as in so many other areas of the world, it was a case of the flag following trade. By the end of the eighteenth century Britain's share of trade with China exceeded that of every other nation put together.

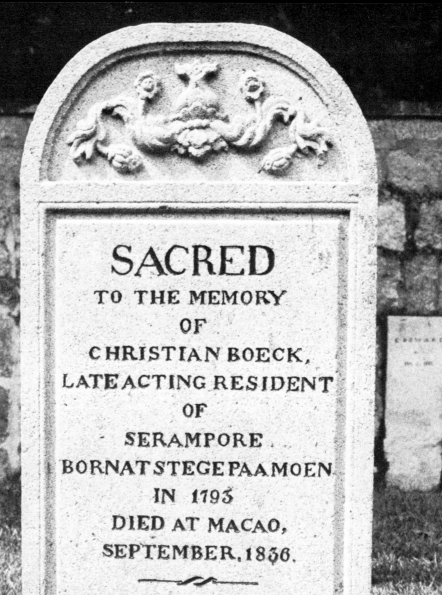

SACRED
TO THE MEMORY
OF
CHRISTIAN BOECK,
LATE ACTING RESIDENT
OF
SERAMPORE
BORN AT STEGE PAA MOEN
IN 1793
DIED AT MACAO,
SEPTEMBER, 1836.

THIS MONUMENT IS
ERECTED BY
JAMES MATHESON,
HIS DANISH MAJESTYS
CONSUL IN CHINA

The China trade was a highly profitable business and the merchants who conducted it lived in grand style: in the dining room of the East India Company factory at Canton there were cut-glass chandeliers hanging from the ceiling and silver candelabra on the tables. Lavish business dinners were a feature of the trader's life. The young William Hickey (after whom the gossip column is named) visited Canton in 1769 and was a guest at a dinner organised by one of the richest of the Cohong merchants. Out of deference to their visitors European food was served and the Chinese hosts politely wrestled with knives and forks. The best European wines were served. The following night Hickey and his compatriots in turn played host and served Chinese food, which Hickey loved: 'Victuals supremely good', he noted in his diary. Despite the profits and the grand style of life, the traders found the restrictions on them irksome. No foreigner was allowed to live in China. After they had completed their trading, they had to retire to the Portuguese colony of Macau, at the mouth of the Pearl river which led up to Canton. With so many foreign seamen congregated in a few seaports, fights were inevitable. The Chinese customs relating to crime and punishment insisted that the foreign community as a whole suffered if one seaman started a brawl. No distinction was made between nationalities and the concept of individual guilt did not enter into it; the entire community was to blame for any incident. Finally, the Chinese custom of extracting 'squeeze'—an arbitrary sum of money levied on a trader to allow his trade to continue—was a continual irritant to the merchants.

For their part, the Chinese found that trade with the West brought an unforeseen problem. The original traders had been obliged to pay for Chinese products in silver, as there were no Western goods which the Chinese wanted. The result had been a flow of silver into China. The traders finally hit on a way of reversing this rather expensive flow—and filling their ships on both legs of the journey. British India produced tons and tons of opium for which there was almost no outlet. No one knows who first thought of bringing this product into China, but by the end of the eighteenth century the trade was well established. Traders were undeterred by the fact that opium was illegal in China and the vice spread rapidly. It started, as drugs tend to, with the young men of good families—then others took up the habit. By the 1830s the number of addicts was estimated at between four and twelve million people—a vast market which the traders were only too happy to exploit. It reversed the flow of silver and China was soon running a massive trade deficit to pay for this new addiction.

In consequence, the implications of the China trade became equally important to the governments of both sides. If the British and other Western nations were concerned to see their trade conducted under conditions of reasonable security and stability, the Chinese for their part wished to halt the flow of opium or, as they called it, 'foreign mud' into China; a flow which they saw as corrupting the nation. In 1836 the Chinese Emperor appointed Lin Tse Hsu as commissioner in Canton and charged him with the unenviable task of ending the opium trade. Shipments of opium from India had increased six-fold over the previous forty years and the opium trade was now an important part of the economy of British India.

Macau tombstone. To get into China, James Matheson had to use diplomatic cover.

The Chinese view was that what the British had started, they could stop. It was—and still is—the view of the Chinese government that Britain had corrupted Chinese minds by introducing the habit of opium smoking. The fact that many Chinese engaged in the trade as middlemen—and profited vastly from it—was neither here nor there. As Commissioner Lin put it in a letter to Queen Victoria in 1839, 'this noxious article is the clandestine manufacture of artful schemers under the domination of your honourable nation'. The British government's attitude was at best equivocal. Though, as the Chinese pointed out, opium was illegal in Britain, public opinion did not hold any particular views with regard to drug taking, and ministers tended to include the whole moral question of opium under the vague heading of the protection of free trade.

William Jardine and James Matheson—founders of Jardine Matheson, the oldest established company in Hong Kong.

Free trade had been a central tenet of British foreign policy since the beginning of the eighteenth century. Economic growth had been greatly stimulated by breaking into the trading markets of Central and South America, Africa and the Mediterranean. Breaking down restrictions on trade brought Britain enormous benefits in terms of wealth and employment, and, as she developed as a major trading power, the political necessity of protecting that freedom increased. Opium was seen as product of free trade like any other.

In public Lord Palmerston, the British Foreign Secretary, accepted the Chinese right to ban opium imports but would not accept that in so doing the queen's subjects should be, 'treated with violence. When wrong was done to them, she would see they obtained redress.' In private, Lord Palmerston had rather different views. In a Foreign Office memorandum of 1841 to the British negotiators with China, he stated:

> I have to instruct you to make some arrangements with the Chinese Government for the admission of opium into China, as an article of lawful commerce . . . You will point out that it is scarcely possible that a permanent good understanding can be maintained between the two governments if the opium trade be allowed to remain upon its present [illegal] footing.

In reality the British view was that if the people of China wished to buy opium no one had any business standing between them and their vices.

In such circumstances conflict was inevitable. Commissioner Lin precipitated matters by seizing 20,000 chests of opium from the foreign factories in Canton and destroying them. The traders promptly demanded compensation. While this was under discussion with Captain Elliot, the British government's Superintendent of Trade in China, a further incident sparked off open conflict. On 7 July 1839 a party of British and American sailors went ashore at Kowloon and became involved in a drunken brawl with villagers. One Chinese was killed. Commissioner Lin demanded that those responsible be handed over. Elliot tried to placate him by placing the seamen on trial and imprisoning them. Unappeased, Lin occupied Macau, the Portuguese trading base opposite Hong Kong from which the British opium traders operated. The traders were incensed and demanded action in response. Lord Palmerston sent the Chinese an ultimatum, demanding compensation for the lost opium and secure conditions for British trade in the future. The Chinese did nothing and fifteen warships and 5,000 troops were dispatched to enforce the ultimatum.

In the war that followed China discovered one of the real gaps between East and West—that of technology. Despite being outnumbered on every occasion, the well-equipped British were able to defeat the ill-organised Chinese forces with ease. The British imposed a blockade on Canton, Amoy, Ningpo and the mouth of the Yangtze River. The island of Chusan, one hundred miles southeast of Shanghai, was captured by British troops, and a landing was made on the mainland. Alarmed, the Chinese offered to negotiate, but the extent of British demands resulted in a stalemate. The Chinese were forced back to the negotiating table by the British capture of strategic forts guarding the river entrance to Canton. On 20 January 1841 the Chinese conceded: trade at Canton was to be reopened and $6 million paid in indemnity for the lost opium. In addition, and in excess of his original instructions, the British negotiator forced China to cede Hong Kong island and its harbour permanently to Britain. This convention was repudiated by both sides almost immediately, which led to renewed conflict. The Treaty of Nanking in 1842, which concluded the First Opium War, contained substantially the same terms—more ports were opened to trade and the indemnity was increased to $21 million in order that the

The Honourable Merchants

The establishment of Hong Kong owes much to the activities of nineteenth-century opium traders. It was they who effectively dominated British foreign policy towards China. The largest and most significant of the China trading companies was Jardine Matheson, known as 'The Princely Hong'. Its partners were known as 'Tai Pans', the Chinese for 'great manager'. The two founders—William Jardine and James Matheson—were respected and feared along the China coast. Jardine was known to awe-struck Chinese as the 'iron-headed rat'. He was a ruthless businessman with little patience for fools. It is recorded that in his office there was only one chair (needless to say his), so as to encourage visitors to conclude their business quickly. He was a legendary hard worker, often staying at his desk till two or three o'clock in the morning. His partner, James Matheson, was a more affable character, described by one contemporary as 'a gentleman of great suavity of manner and the impersonation of benevolence'. If the profits of opium trading, upon which the two built their fortunes, were enormous, so too was the scale of their munificent gifts: when Matheson left Macau and took his base to Hong Kong, he gave the governor $5,000 for charitable use.

Both were influential in the events leading up to the foundation of Hong Kong. While Jardine, in London, put pressure on Lord Palmerston at the Foreign Office, Matheson was in Hong Kong, advising the British plenipotentiary in his dealings with the Chinese. It was Matheson who persuaded the British government that a permanent base was needed on the China coast, Matheson who picked on Hong Kong, Matheson who erected the new colony's first permanent building.

Jardine Matheson has remained synonymous with Hong Kong. Today their headquarters at the Connaught Centre dominates the skyline of Hong Kong, and the chairman of Jardine Matheson still carries the ancient title of 'The Honourable Merchant'. It seems strange that such a title should be born by the head of a firm that made its fortune from drug smuggling, but Jardine and Matheson had a reputation as honest traders amongst their contemporaries. They were careful to ensure that their ships carried only the best Bengal Opium and were the first to complain if any trader sold adulterated products: 'I would in almost every case', wrote Matheson, 'attribute it to disintegrity in the part of the agent . . . the article having for some time been attended with such large profits as to hold out more than common temptation to the weak passions of our nature.'

Chinese should pay for the war as well as the lost opium. Hong Kong remained tacked on the end.

For the British the real significance of the 1839–42 war had been that it had formalised relations with China and established a basis on which trade could continue. The acquisition of Hong Kong against orders met with disapproval at home. Indeed Lord Palmerston scornfully described Hong Kong in a famous line as 'a barren island with scarcely a house on it'. No one in London could understand why the British negotiator had bothered himself with a place that had no conceivable value—it was not even on the mainland of China—and which would probably cost money to defend.

The Chinese on the other hand did regard the ceding of Hong Kong as important—not for its strategic or economic value (which was nil) but because it was a part of Chinese soil. It was not seen as a permanent gift: the Chinese official in charge of the negotiations, in seeking to explain to the Emperor why a part of China had been given away, said that he would 'seek another occasion for attacking and destroying them [the British] at Hong Kong, and thus restore the ancient territory.' Indeed the Chinese never disguised their intention of removing the British from Hong Kong when a suitable opportunity arose. During the Second Opium War they resorted to an interesting form of harrassment designed to warn the barbarians. Chinese government officials enterprisingly tried to poison the governor of Hong Kong with arsenic. The dose administered was far too high and the intended victims vomited up their food long before the poison could take effect.

Chinese resentment of the humiliating conditions imposed on them after the First Opium War remained: they were powerless to stop the flourishing opium trade. On the Western side, there were resentments too: the Chinese appeared to be dragging their feet on the opening up of trade, as agreed under the Treaty of Nanking. Attempts by the Chinese to keep the barbarian at bay resulted in a series of incidents. In October 1856 the Chinese seized the crew of a British schooner, the *Arrow*. The Chinese justified their action by claiming that three of the seamen were notorious Chinese pirates. The British demanded the release of the prisoners, an apology and a guarantee that the British flag would in future be respected. The Chinese refused and war broke out. The British found an ally in the French, who also wished to force the opening up of China to trade, and could claim similar insults to their flag. The military campaigns of the Second Opium War and the Third Opium War which followed immediately on its heels, were similar to those of the 1839–42 war, but more protracted. British and French forces seized Canton in 1858, and in 1860 a combined force of some 18,000 men landed further north and marched on Peking. By the beginning of October 1860, the allies had fought their way to the gates of Peking, sacking the Emperor's Summer Palace en route; on 24 October 1860, Lord Elgin, the British plenipotentiary, accepted the Chinese surrender in the Hall of Ceremonies.

The war—and the trade behind it—were not without opponents at home in Britain. The Liberal, Gladstone, amongst others, saw a sharp contrast between the ideals Britain professed to hold and the action she was prepared to take in order to safeguard her interests: 'We the enlightened and civilised Christians are pursuing objectives at variance both with justice and with religion.' He failed to see why the Union Jack should be 'hoisted to protect an infamous contraband trade'. Lord Palmerston would not be drawn, preferring instead to attack the Chinese as 'insolent barbarians', and, in so doing, demonstrated a strange reversal of roles in which the language of the Chinese imperial court became the coinage of the British parliament!

Under the terms of the Treaty of Peking in 1860, more ports were opened to trade and a British ambassador was sent to Peking. A further clause ceded Kowloon to the British colony of Hong Kong: both sides of the harbour were now in British hands.

Peace was established on a basis that was to last for forty years. But it was the peace of the powerful over the weak, a fact that China was never to forget; the nineteenth-century treaties extorted from China at the point of a bayonet are regarded by the Chinese today as invalid. The British were never morally sure of their right to control chunks of China—the so-called treaty ports at which trading was allowed, and where British and not Chinese writ ran. In the twentieth century Britain came to regard these provisions as an unfortunate hangover from history and took the opportunity of alliance with China during the Second World War to renounce the principle of treaty ports. They did not however renounce Hong Kong, which to this day remains the last legacy of the unequal treaties of the nineteenth century. That is the fundamental fact of the colony's past which stays to haunt it in the years to come. It was a product of the bloody exercise of military strength; Hong Kong was and is a part of China.

The early settlers of Hong Kong found it virtually uninhabited, incapable of supporting life and ridden with disease. Like Lord Palmerston they found it hard to see this new acquisition of empire as being of any value whatsoever. It had been acquired to provide the traders with a secure base from which to manage their operations (see p. 32). In this they had been backed by the Royal Navy, which wanted a good deep-water port as a base. Hong Kong means 'Fragrant Harbour' in Chinese—that it was one of the best harbours in the world no one could dispute; of its fragrancy not all were agreed.

Hong Kong's early colonial history was somewhat shabby. Aside from its unhealthy climate the island swiftly attracted a motley collection of smugglers, opium dealers and criminals on the run from Chinese law. Even the traders who had been so keen on Hong Kong as a base preferred to spend their time on the mainland, supervising trade. One visitor described the Chinese residents as 'the last dregs of native society' while noting that the British of Hong Kong were hated by the Chinese for their 'moral improprieties and insolent behaviour'. In the course of time Hong Kong became a more respectable place. The population rose rapidly from 5,000 before the British arrived to 125,000 by 1865 and a quarter of a million by 1898. One thing the Chinese government had not bargained on was that Chinese people would be willing to go and live under the domination of Western devils. Meanwhile, Hong Kong's commercial importance grew as the centre

Hong Kong Harbour in about 1850.

of Asia's rapidly increasing entrepôt trade. By the end of the nineteenth century almost half of China's trade came via Hong Kong and the colony's total trade was valued annually at £50 million.

If there is a lesson to be learnt from the past, it is that the colony remains valuable to Britain only as long as it remains valuable to her traders. As far as the Chinese are concerned nothing has altered—indeed the nationalist government of China, which took power after the revolution of 1911, and the communist rulers of modern China have repeated their desire to eliminate the last remnant of the unequal treaties of the nineteenth century. It is a demand that is voiced with varying degrees of intensity, depending on what other problems China is facing at the time—but it is a demand that will not go away.

The delicate balancing act between China and Britain has become another of the spurs which drives Hong Kong on. It was perhaps best summed up by a petition from the traders of Hong Kong to Queen Victoria in 1894:

> Hong Kong has attained to its almost unequalled commercial position through the enterprise, skill and energy of British merchants, traders and shipowners; through the labours of Her Majesty's subjects who have spent their lives and employed their capital on its shores; through the expenditure of many millions of dollars in roads, streets and bridges; in building public and private; in extensive reclamations; in

35

docks, piers and wharves; and last but not least, in manufactures of great and increasing value. The prosperity of the colony can best be maintained by the unremitting exertions and self-sacrifice of your petitioners, and the valuable co-operation and support of the Chinese, and only by the continuance of Hong Kong as a free port.

It is a description of Hong Kong that could hardly be bettered, but one that could conceivably become its epitaph as well.

CHAPTER FOUR

THE POWER HOUSE

On 7 December 1941, Hong Kong's most prestigious hotel, the Peninsular, played host to a glittering social event when the Hong Kong Chinese Women's Clubs held a fancy-dress ball in aid of British and Chinese bomber funds. The Rose Room and the roof garden of the hotel were crowded with ingenious costumes, and the affair was described by the *South China Morning Post*, Hong Kong's English language newspaper, as 'a brilliant function'. The following day the Japanese invaded Hong Kong. There was little resistance from the ill-prepared and weak British military forces, and on Christmas Day 1941, the British governor of Hong Kong and the garrison commander surrendered unconditionally to the Japanese in a short ceremony at the Peninsular. The collapse of British power was, as in Singapore, swift and total. Hong Kong was left to the mercy of its invaders.

The British surrender in 1941 taught Hong Kong a lesson it has never forgotten—that it cannot rely on anyone; one must be self-sufficient at all times, trusting only to one's own resources and ingenuity. The survivors in this world are those who have no illusions about their enemies—or their friends. The lesson has been taught repeatedly since. Hong Kong has learnt the hazards of its strange status. It is almost unique in the world—a major world economy, yet not an independent nation, with the ability to look after itself. For Hong Kong, self-reliance is not a desirable virtue, it is a cruel necessity.

The Hong Kong over which the Union Jack was raised again on 30 August 1945 was a devastated shambles. In 1941 it had a population of 1,600,000; by 1945 that figure had been reduced to less than half a million as a direct result of the Japanese occupation. Hong Kong had been of little use to the Japanese war strategy; it had no part to play in the much-vaunted Far East Asia Co. Prosperity Sphere, and during the Occupation was treated accordingly as a piece of enemy territory to be looted and ransacked at will. Many of its people were forced to return to China in search of food, as the Japanese were reluctant to feed what they regarded as useless mouths. Hong Kong in 1945 had a population that was debilitated by disease, an economy crippled by war, and hardly a building left intact.

The long struggle back to something resembling normality had hardly begun when another event outside Hong Kong's control knocked the economy sideways. Hong Kong had re-established itself as a China trader in the immediate post-war years. This trade was destroyed overnight in 1951.

The advent to power in mainland China of a communist government in 1949 meant a China dedicated to playing a more active role in the politics of Asia. An opportunity soon offered itself. On 24 June 1950, North Korean troops invaded South Korea. The Security Council of the United Nations demanded the support of UN members 'to repel armed attack and restore international peace'. Troops from a number of UN member states, including the United States and Britain, were sent to enforce the resolution. On 8 October, as they advanced against the North Koreans, UN forces crossed the 38th Parallel, the border between North and South Korea. In response, China intervened on behalf of the North Koreans. Within three weeks, Chinese forces were engaged on the ground alongside North Korean units, helping them to repel the advancing UN troops. Chinese refusal to withdraw resulted in a UN resolution on 31 January 1951 condemning China for 'aggression in Korea'. In support of the UN resolution, mandatory sanctions were imposed, banning the export of a wide range of strategic commodities to the People's Republic. As the dependency of a loyal member of the United Nations, Hong Kong had no choice but to comply with the sanctions.

It was a major disaster for the colony. Nearly one-third of Hong Kong's foreign trade earnings vanished overnight. Within five years trade with China dropped to one-tenth of its 1951 level. It looked as if the whole of the colony's post-war economic recovery would evaporate, as if the colony might return to the shambles it had been in 1945. In fact that blow has been described as 'disastrous but not catastrophic', for it forced Hong Kong to rethink its role in the world economy. Historically a centre for China trading and an entrepôt port through which other people's goods passed, Hong Kong now broadened the base of its economy by moving into manufacturing on its own account. Before the war, manufacturing had been insignificant in Hong Kong—by the late 1950s it had become the bedrock of the economy.

There was another factor pushing Hong Kong towards industrialisation. At the end of the war, those who had been forced to leave Hong Kong returned, looking for employment. Within a few years they were joined by refugees from the communist takeover of China. Many of these were entrepreneurs or skilled workers—people who had worked in the factories of Shanghai before the revolution, and who were keen to get away from the state-controlled economy of communist China. They brought with them industrial and organisational skills, which in effect gave Hong Kong a transplant of industry. The industrial growth rate was rapid. Between 1950 and 1980 the number of manufacturing establishments in Hong Kong increased thirty times.

The product which turned Hong Kong into a manufacturing nation was that which had provided the basis for Britain's industrial revolution—textiles. In part this was an accident of history, since many of the Chinese refugees had previously worked in the textile factories of Shanghai. In addition textiles has always been the classic 'start up' industry; the product is simple, the investment small, the end result easy to market. By 1973 Hong Kong had become the world's leading exporter of textile products; a

Hong Kong from the peak — daytime; overleaf — night-time.

The Man With the Golden Grin

Woo Hon Fai is the sort of person Hong Kongers point to as the example of a man who has pulled himself up by his bootstraps. His father was a silk merchant in South China who emigrated in 1937 during the Japanese invasion and came to Hong Kong, bringing his young son with him. Cynical Hong Kongers say the family arrived in Hong Kong with 'nothing but the shirts on their backs—and a suitcase full of gold'. Today Mr Woo is one of the pillars of Hong Kong's business community, with fingers in almost every pie. His business card is hardly big enough for all his titles: President of the Chinese Gold and Silver Exchange Society, Chairman of the Kam Ngan Stock Exchange, Vice-Chairman of the Hong Kong Commodity Exchange, Vice-Chairman of the Real Estate Developers Association of Hong Kong—to say nothing of chairman of the new unified Stock Exchange of Hong Kong, a post to which he has recently been elected.

Listening to Mr Woo you hear the authentic tones of the mid-Victorian British capitalist—a Samuel Smiles in Chinese.

We Chinese are a diligent lot—we are also persistent and have a talent as entrepreneurs. Most of Hong Kong's successful people live by hard work and do not give up easily. If we don't succeed we try again. We often work long hours—I believe our success lies in our willingness to work. That is the difference between you and us.

Questioned about Hong Kong's future, Mr Woo snorts in indignation:

Our problem is not China but Britain. China needs Hong Kong the way it is. Why do I say our problem is Britain? We have a different culture and set of values to you—take British labour laws for example. No doubt due to the influence of British thinking, we were forced to accept regulations giving our workforce seven continuous days off a year.

You could say that Mr Woo was a conservative. He won election to the chairmanship of the Stock Exchange in a hotly contested ballot on a platform of minimum government regulation and a continuing ban on foreign brokers in Hong Kong. He hastens to point out that he's not anti-British: 'You let our brokers work on the London Stock Exchange and we'll let yours in here.' But he is vigorous in his defence of Chinese businessmen against the encroachments of government: 'A free market should be allowed to develop without being hindered unnecessarily. The fewer regulations the better.' Given Mr Woo's track record, that is a battle he seems likely to win.

position it has retained. At its peak in the 1960s, textiles dominated Hong Kong's foreign trade, providing 70 per cent of exports. In 1981 textiles still represented far and away the largest sector, employing 40 per cent of the workforce and making up 42 per cent of exports.

Woo Hon Fai—gold dealer, stockbroker, property developer.

There is something awe-inspiring about the sheer scale of the textile industry in Hong Kong. The Smart Shirt company in Kowloon is a case in point. It occupies a six-storey block on an industrial estate in Kwun Tong. One of its plants turns out 60,000 shirts a day. The company as a group claims to make 1.6 million dozen shirts every year (that's about one shirt for every adult in Britain) using 2,300 machines and 4,500 workers. The proprietor, Mr Ying, used to be in the shirt business in Shanghai, and now exports his shirts all over the world, mostly to America, though some come to Britain. The pace of work in this palace of shirtmaking is exhausting. The girl who works the machine making cuffs turns them out at about one every six seconds. Her work rate is determined by the relentless rhythmic pace of the stitching machine: it opens its jaws every six seconds for a fresh offering of two slices of cloth with stiffener in between. Elsewhere in the factory, buttons are sewn on in four seconds, sleeves take about seven seconds, collars another six, labels only three. The women in the folding section, packaging the shirts for transit, move so fast it is almost impossible to see their hands making individual moves—taking about twenty-five seconds, they insert the pins, cellophane and cardboard that take so long to remove when you buy the shirt. Smart Shirts is one of many companies at the bulk end of the market. It is intensely competitive and the emphasis is on good quality, low price and fast delivery. You can only do that if you have huge volume, which in turn means selling vast numbers of shirts.

It is Hong Kong's success at marketing its huge volume output that has caused problems. Importing countries, including Britain and the United States, have watched in dismay as this efficient and competitive industry has swooped in on their home markets, threatening domestic producers. The developed nations have retaliated with restrictions and limitations on imports. The means employed for squeezing Hong Kong and other low-cost textile producers has been the General Agreement on Trade and Tarriffs (GATT). This was originally negotiated in 1948 as a way of freeing world trade from the restrictions imposed during the depression of the pre-war years. In the 1930s individual countries had imposed restrictions on a large number of imported products as a way of protecting home industries—which stultified world trade and effectively prevented any chance of an economic revival. After the first burst of tariff-cutting enthusiasm in the 1950s and 1960s, GATT became a restrictive agreement. It is now a forum in which the 'haves'—the industrialised nations—can enforce their wishes on the 'have nots'—the developing countries.

Britain was the first country to impose limitations on textile exports from Hong Kong in 1959. This was followed in 1974 by a seemingly innocuous agreement within GATT called the Multi Fibre Arrangement (MFA). The 'arrangement' limited the growth rate of less developed countries' exports of textiles to the developed world. It was intended as a temporary measure, to relieve the pressure on European and American domestic manufactures, but, like many other temporary measures, it seems to have become permanent. In 1977 there was a further round of MFA talks and more restrictions were imposed. Currently the MFA is being renewed yet again, in a series of negotiations that Hong Kong's Commissioner of Trade, Lawrence Mills, has described as 'long, hard and bloody'. Further tightening of quotas is inevitable.

The main charge against Hong Kong and other developing countries has been that of unfair competition. On one count that is manifestly true. No European or American would put up with the working conditions in a factory like Smart Shirts. In Hong Kong the level of workers' expectations is lower. On other aspects of unfair competition, the case is less strong. Unlike America, Hong Kong does not subsidise its textile industry with cheap raw materials; unlike Britain, there is no subsidy to industry from government; and Hong Kong's domestic industry is given no protection whatsoever from foreign imports. Furthermore, Hong Kong disputes that it is imports from developing countries that are doing the damage and the facts would seem to support this argument. A study in Britain on the decline of employment in the textile industry placed most of the blame on productivity improvements not imports. Between 1970 and 1975, 110,000 jobs were lost in textiles in the UK: productivity improvements caused two-thirds of those jobs to go, competition from imports only one-third. And the imports which seem to have done most of the damage are not those from places like Hong Kong. These accounted for less than one-sixth of the total loss of jobs. The main damage has been done by imports from other developed countries like Italy and the United States. Managers like Lydia Dunn, who runs her own textile company in Hong Kong, point out that while Hong Kong has had restrictions on its exports for nearly twenty years, the United States has been able to get away with an ever-increasing share of the European market:

> We are unable to grow by more than 3–4 per cent a year in our exports, whereas countries like America are unrestricted. In 1980 the growth rate of US textile imports to the Common Market was huge: sweaters, up 16 per cent; knitted shirts up 98 per cent; synthetic fibres up 34 per cent. Now why not blame them? Why always put the blame on Hong Kong?

Lydia Dunn's question is rhetorical since she already knows the answer. Hong Kong is a small place with very little international clout. The United States, on the other hand, is a superpower in economic as well as political terms. America can speak up for itself while Hong Kong can't. Hong Kong's external relations, which include trade, are handled by Britain. Any complaints about unfair treatment, therefore, are dealt with by a country that believes it has suffered at the hands of Hong Kong's successful businessmen. The dual role of Britain, at once Hong Kong's protector at the negotiating table and business competitor, causes severe strains in the relationship between colony and mother country. 'We don't feel,' concludes Lydia Dunn, 'that in the last few years we in the textile industry in Hong Kong have had the support from Britain we should have had'. Civil servant Bill Dorward describes the tangled position of Britain and Hong Kong with masterly understatement as

> a very complicated situation. I won't say there haven't ever been conflicts with Britain in trade terms, but we do keep these within the family. We don't argue on the public stage when we do have conflicts. But there is clearly a divergence of view. Hong Kong is after all among the top twenty trading entities in the world. So we have our own row to hoe.

It is not difficult to detect, in conversation with the Foreign Office in London, the order of priorities in trade talks. After all, unemployed British textile workers have votes, while Hong Kongers don't. Humphrey Atkins, formerly a minister at the Foreign Office, had the job of negotiating the latest round of the MFA on behalf of Britain and Hong Kong. He made his priorities quite clear:

> One thing we can't forget is that over the last eighteen months 150,000 jobs have been lost in the UK in the textile industry, and this is something we must keep in mind when we are deciding what are the best arrangements for importing low-cost textiles.

But Mr Atkins went on to sugar the pill of tighter restrictions:

> The new arrangement will be a voluntary one, which both sides agree is the best way to proceed. Hong Kong will have a guaranteed amount they can export to the European community, and they will be able to plan on that basis.

These words were received with little surprise or anger in Hong Kong. They know that British political realities do not include unemployment in the Hong Kong textile industry. Though Hong Kongers do not question the detailed arrangements made under MFA, which they regard as less of an evil than unilateral embargoes, they do question the principle behind it. Lydia Dunn wonders who benefits from protectionism:

> In the final analysis it's the consumer who suffers most. The consumer is denied the opportunity to spend his money on the product which offers the most value. We, the exporting countries, suffer because our growth rates are arbitrarily and artificially restrained; and you, the importing countries, also suffer because you misallocate resources, you protect inefficient industries, you stop people moving into more efficient and more profitable industries. We all lose out.

That is a very clear statement of the Hong Kong view of trade, and one which comes from the heart. While other countries preach free trade in public, in private they practise protectionism. By contrast, Hong Kong not only believes in free trade but puts that belief into practice. Says Hong Kong and Shanghai Bank chairman, Michael Sandberg,

> We're rather different from most places in that we actually encourage dumping. If we have steel bars dumped on us that makes our construction costs lower, if we have sugar dumped on us that makes the housewife's bill lower. And those who've been involved in sugar refining or making steel bars have got to pull their belts in a little tighter.

With so large a proportion of its gross domestic product dependant on exports, Hong Kong's standard of living is heavily dependant on free trade. But that trade looks like being increasingly circumscribed by quotas in the future. Yesterday's temporary quota is today's permanent restriction. The response of the textile trade to such limitations on the growth of its volume production has been to move into specialised and quota-free products. That has effectively meant moving up-market into quality goods.

The move up-market has not been helped by Hong Kong's image as the maker of the cheap and cheerful—an image which Hong Kong contends is now quite false. 'I think Britain is probably the only place in the world where the "Made in Hong Kong" label is still faintly unsavoury,' says Bill Dorward, Hong Kong's Director of Trade and Industry. 'The "Made in Hong Kong" label elsewhere is a prestige label. It means quality.'

Quality means using materials like silk. A typical factory in the new mould of Hong Kong textiles is Lim Ying Ying products in Kowloon. It is as crowded and as energetic a workplace as Smart Shirts, but a lot quieter. The products are handmade, each with an individual design which must be carefully cut out and sewn by one worker with needle and thread. The emphasis is on good design, patient workmanship, skilful handling and attention to detail. Lim Ying Ying's client list is impressive; it includes Harrods in London and Saks Fifth Avenue in New York. Designers have in turn discovered Hong Kong; the factory makes ready-to-wear designs for Christian Dior.

Street toy seller—one image of Hong Kong goods.

Hong Kong is vigorously promoting its new image abroad. In 1981 European fashion journalists gave a warm welcome to a large display organised by the Hong Kong Trade Development Council at the chic *Prêt-à-Porter* show in Paris. The show is widely regarded as the most important fashion display in the world, and over 150,000 buyers from the world's rag trade were present. The buyers were impressed and there is no doubt that this end of the textile business can sustain growth. But it is a very small part of the overall business and Hong Kongers who pin the hopes of the textile industry on fashion goods are being over-optimistic. There isn't a volume market for high-fashion goods and most Hong Kong textile companies just aren't capable of providing the sort of quality goods the top end of the business requires. For those companies who have been able to make the transition, it has been a good move. Besides avoiding quota restrictions, the profit margin on quality goods is much better. Mass-produced goods rely on volume not mark-up for their profitability. Quality goods can afford better margins.

The mass production end of Hong Kong's textile industry faces a further problem. It is not only suffering restrictions on exports to the developed countries but is also under attack from rivals in the less developed world. Hungrier and leaner rivals like Sri Lanka, which up till now have had no industry at all, have also chosen textiles as their route to industrialisation. They have ample supplies of labour prepared to accept lower wages and worse working conditions than those in Hong Kong. Bill Dorward describes it as a 'lobster quadrille', as the hungry nations of Asia vie with each other to undercut the market leaders in the battle for world trade.

Hong Kong is currently the market leader in Asia, relatively speaking the 'have' in an area of 'have nots'. Ironically, it is facing the same problem today that confronted Britain in the early 1950s. The government's Financial Secretary, John Bremridge, remembers living in Japan then:

> Trade unionists used to come over from Britain and say these people are operating on miserable pay scales, it's unfair competition. I can remember saying then, what are you going to say when they are paid more than you? Well I think the same thing is true in Hong Kong.

He sees the solution as clear:

> Countries with lower wage scales than us are taking over from us at the bottom of the pile. We have to go up-market in everything. Frankly we have no other way to go because either we're successful or we die. This spurs one on.

For those who are left behind in the scramble to go up-market, there will be no help from government.

> I've got the greatest sympathy for them. Nothing can be worse than running an industry at the wrong end of the spectrum, like the cheap end of the textile business, at a time of problems abroad and protectionism. It's terrible. But the fact remains that these people ought to go down. They should not be supported by government.

Hard words from Bremridge, but a recognition of the central reality of Hong Kong—that you live or die by your own efforts, by whether you have the will to adapt.

The importance of the textile industry will inevitably decline. Hong Kong's businessmen are reacting to the threat of diminishing markets and increased competition by switching to products too sophisticated for their more primitive rivals. Plastics, toys, electronics and photographic equipment are becoming more important in Hong Kong's manufacturing sector. Diversification has had to be into light industrial products like these, for Hong Kong doesn't have either the space, the skills or the manufacturing capacity for the sort of sophisticated products that large, developed countries can produce.

The shift into light industrial products has not been without its problems. The digital watch industry is a case in point. No sooner had one company started making them—under licence from Japan—than every company in Hong Kong with any electronics skills moved into the business. The market boomed, and then collapsed almost as suddenly. Price-cutting made this supposedly up-market product largely unprofitable, and Hong Kong found itself facing protectionist pressures, much as it had done with textiles. In October 1981 the French government decided that in order to protect its domestic watch industry, it would have to impose restrictions on the import of watches from Hong Kong. At the time trade was running at an estimated 8 million watches a year. Hong Kong traders were informed that for the period from October 1981 to December 1982, no more than 5.5 million digital watches might be imported into France.

To compound the offence the French government didn't even bother to tell the Hong Kong government direct. Officials in Hong Kong only found out when they read press reports. Their reaction was a masterpiece of understatement. They described the French action as 'discourteous, to say the least'. Retaliation was pointless—France's main export to Hong Kong is brandy, of which Hong Kong drinks more per head of the population than anywhere else in the world. It is widely believed among the Chinese to have aphrodisiac powers; a ban would thus be unlikely to have much popular support in Hong Kong. Action on the diplomatic level was also muted. It required the support of Britain as Hong Kong's sponsoring power. With Britain embroiled in interminable disputes with France on the Common Market budget, a small item like quotas on Hong Kong would count for little. Lydia Dunn is gloomy about the future: 'I still like to believe that major trading countries would not disregard the rule of law casually. We have to believe that—otherwise we'll be back in jungle warfare again.'

In an attempt to diversify away from dependence on manufacturing, Hong Kong has set its sights on becoming the financial capital of Asia. As trade in Asia has expanded, so has the need for all the paraphernalia of trade—foreign exchange, insurance, ship chartering, international banking and the like. In the struggle to lead the field in Asia, Hong Kong is in direct competition with its fellow city state of Singapore and, for the time being at least, appears to be winning. The financial sector is growing at the rate of 17 per cent a year. By the end of 1981 there were 123 licensed banks in Hong Kong with 1,301 branches. Of these, 89 were foreign based. In addition, there were 121 representative branches of other foreign banks. The government adopts an open-door policy towards banking, with few rules and minimal interference. One banker describes the atmosphere thus:

It is a very free market. The philosophy of Hong Kong is laissez faire, which I interpret to mean minimal regulation. There's no form of exchange control, which was abolished in the early seventies. It's a place to come and establish an office, offer a service which is in demand, make money, pay your taxes and remit your profits.

Foreign exchange dealing room, Sun Hung Kai Finance.

The tax on profits is less than half the amount levied in Britain.

The bankers have responded to this open attitude by turning Hong Kong into one of the world's major centres of international banking. Hong Kong bankers are beginning to win corporate banking custom from London and New York—until now unchallenged in that very specialised and highly profitable business. A few years ago there was virtually no foreign exchange dealing in Hong Kong beyond that strictly required for local trade. Today Hong Kong is called the 'engine room' of the Far Eastern foreign exchange market because of the amounts of money it handles. By exploiting the time differences in the global business clock, Hong Kong has managed to slot itself into the gap that used to exist after San Francisco bankers went to bed and before the Middle East and London markets opened. Now you can carry on dealing for almost 24 hours of the day round the world. At 10 a.m. in Hong Kong, the Japanese are breaking for lunch, the Australians are about to come into the market, London is asleep, New York dealers are on their way home after yesterday's dealing and San Francisco is winding down.

Much of the world's investment cash is finding its way into Hong Kong too. Today there are few London or New York stockbrokers who do not offer clients a portfolio of investments in Hong Kong. Ten years ago no one would have thought of investing in the unknown quantity of Asia. Today South East Asia offers the best return on investment anywhere in the world. A Hong Kong company would be regarded as losing money if it made less than a 20 per cent return on capital each year, a figure that few

47

A Sting in the Tael

Hong Kong's Gold Market looks like a cross between the Eton Wall game and Thai boxing. It's housed in a small building in Mercer Street, on the western end of the central area of Hong Kong. Inside is a small square room, with a raised step all round the edge. Banks of telephones hang on the wall. The centre of the floor is the trading ring and it's only the very bold who dare to enter the ring while trading is in progress. It is what is known officially as 'market by open outcry'. The floor is full of traders gesticulating wildly with their fingers in the air. Drawing your hand towards you is a signal that you are buying; pushing away that you are selling. The number of fingers you have in the air indicates the number of dollars you are buying or selling above or below the last marked price. At the same time the trader shouts out his offer in Cantonese.

The deal is concluded by physical contact—a tap on the shoulder or a bear hug, depending on how hectic trading is. The dealer's marker follows, writing the details in a book. Along the wall, one of the back-up team shouts the prices down a phone to head office. Trading is in Chinese taels—one tael is roughly equivalent to 1.2 ounces.

It is bedlam; but everyone knows what they're doing and all bargains, once struck, are honoured scrupulously. Virtually none of the buyers and sellers on this market ever see the gold they trade. About 95 per cent of the market's turnover is speculative gold—paper gold which the buyer is obtaining for a gamble. Hong Kong's flourishing jewellery and electronics businesses take the only physical gold that's traded—5 per cent of the total. Ten years ago the gold market was a small local affair—today, after New York and the London/Zurich market, it has the third largest turnover in the world.

Macau, the Portuguese colony forty miles from Hong Kong across the Pearl River, used to be the Far East's unofficial gold centre. Then eight years ago the Hong Kong government lifted the ban on imports of gold and the market took off. It is a classic case of Hong Kong perceiving a gap and exploiting it.

Hong Kong's Gold Exchange in action.

companies in Britain or North America could match.

Much of that money is speculative cash looking for a fast return. Financial Secretary John Bremridge is somewhat unusual among the world's finance ministers in his view of this: 'A lot of people invest in Hong Kong, not for the long run, but to turn a speculative profit. And there's nothing wrong in this at all, in fact we encourage it.' It is no surprise that gold dealing, the most speculative of all businesses, has taken off in Hong Kong. Whereas ten years ago there was only a small local market in the colony, today Hong Kong is the world's third major gold market (see p. 48). Companies who have set up offices here include most of the world's major bullion dealers, who until recently wouldn't have taken Hong Kong seriously as a business centre. As one Hong Kong gold dealer pointed out: 'Once it was always us who were ringing up London to ask the latest gold prices—they didn't want to know about us. Now they do—as often as not, it's they who are ringing us.' One banker put it thus: 'We're no longer a funny little rock with a bunch of coolies squatting on it knitting textiles. We pack a major punch.' But the vision of Hong Kong as an Asiatic Wall Street isn't as simple as that. In the same way that success in industrial manufacturing brought retribution in the form of quotas, so success in the financial and services sector could lead to retaliation. Already Western nations have found to their cost that developing countries like to have key sectors of the economy under national control, and are hostile to unrestrained foreign investment.

The pundits in Hong Kong claim that the financial sector will be the growth area of the next decade, but there is a limit to the number of people who can be employed in it. Hong Kong remains an industrially based economy—a dependence that is looking increasingly unhealthy—and no one in Hong Kong is prepared to invest in the technology of the day after tomorrow. But that sort of investment is essential for the long-term prospects of a mature industrial economy. Hong Kong is in an uncomfortable position, half-way between two worlds. It is not yet a member of the club of rich nations, nor is it any longer one of the world's poor. It is resented for its presumption by the 'haves' and envied for its success by the 'have nots'. It is not a real nation with an independent existence, and it has no means of ensuring that its views are heard.

Put these points to Hong Kongers and they shrug their shoulders. For the moment they are happy to have survived the rigours of the past. John Bremridge again: 'If you look round Hong Kong now, and you remember that in 1945 it was probably the most looted city in the world, it was flat, had a population of 400,000 . . . well, we haven't done too badly, have we?'

CHAPTER FIVE
THE MONOPOLY GAME

Most outsiders' view of Hong Kong is conditioned by that classic of the 1950s, *The World of Suzie Wong*. The portrait that Richard Mason painted of the gentle Chinese bar girls tending to the needs of tired Westerners lives on as the image of Hong Kong. In the 1960s a generation of Americans on rest and recreation from Vietnam scoured the Wanchai district of Hong Kong in search of Suzie. The Wanch, as it used to be known, the waterfront area of Hong Kong, was regarded as the place you used to go for a good time, a rather seedy, slightly rundown part of the world, where you could enjoy yourself without it costing the earth.

Today the Wanchai has changed. The bars are still there, though not in such numbers, and now cater mainly for Japanese businessmen. Girls like Suzie are fighting a rearguard action for survival. They have been caught up in the battle to redevelop the Wanchai. Having redeveloped the central area of Hong Kong—one building has been rebuilt three times since the war—the property men are moving eastwards along the coast of the island into the Wanchai, looking for new redevelopment sites. Many of the buildings are old, low-rise multi-occupancy tenements. They are being replaced with buildings more suitable to the 1980s, high-rise office and apartment blocks. The pace of speculative development has reached fever pitch. On a corner of the Lockhart Road in the Wanchai stands a gaping hole in the ground. A short while ago it was a gleaming new apartment block. No sooner was it finished than the government announced that a new station for the Mass Transit Railway was to be built opposite. The developer promptly applied for—and got—permission to rebuild the apartments as offices. He demolished the building and started again.

The pace of the redevelopment of Hong Kong is as if the whole of the rebuilding of London after the Second World War had been compressed into a decade and a tenth of the space. Construction work goes on at what can only be described as a maniacal pace, often all through the night. In the centre of town in the business district they are rebuilding the Hong Kong and Shanghai Bank's headquarters. To demolish the reinforced concrete of the old foundations required power-driven jack hammers. They started at 7 a.m. and continued until 7 p.m. The noise was deafening. They would have worked longer hours if they could, but Hong Kong's governor, Sir Murray MacLehose, whose mansion is directly up the hill above the site, couldn't get any sleep when they were working round the clock, and

Skyscraper being built—one storey every six days.

requested them to limit hammering to twelve hours a day. Workers on construction sites in Hong Kong are often paid on the basis of bonuses for early completion. With the pressure on the construction industry in Hong Kong, which is working flat out, workers aren't afraid of finishing a job ahead of schedule. There is always more work to go to, and thus no fear of unemployment when a job finishes. One British engineer estimated that the skyscraper he was building would be finished in about one-third of the time it would have taken in the UK. It was going up at the rate of one storey every six days.

The reason for this pace of work is simple. The profits to be reaped are immense. The property men of Hong Kong talk casually in terms of tens of billions of dollars (albeit Hong Kong dollars, of which there are roughly ten to £1 sterling, five to the US dollar). They are the uncrowned kings of Hong Kong's business community and no one else makes the profits or returns the dividends they do. It's all based on rocketing property values. The Hong Kong Land Corporation's Connaught Centre, a massive skyscraper which towers over central Hong Kong, was bought ten years ago for about £28 million. Today it's worth more than ten times that amount. The colony's second largest property company, Cheung Kong, made a profit of about £4 million after tax five years ago; in 1981 the figure was £130 million. Its shares have also risen phenomenally in value. As multi-millionaire chairman Li Ka Shing explains, 'If you had invested ten dollars in my company in 1972, today your shares would be worth two hundred and fifty dollars—

and besides that you would have received ten times the dividend of 1972.'

For developers like Li Ka Shing and Trevor Bedford, chairman of the Hong Kong Land Corporation, Hong Kong is a real-life game of Monopoly. On the board game, the highest return comes from having an hotel on a site. Today hotels aren't as valuable as office blocks. The Hilton Hotel, one of many properties owned by Li Ka Shing's company, isn't regarded by him as a particularly profitable investment, despite the fact that it is one of Hong Kong's most expensive luxury hotels. Li describes it as 'a social service to the community', which is a strange description of a place that costs about £80 a night (excluding breakfast). The underlying economics of hotel operation mean that although the average square foot of space in the Hilton earns more each year than the average square foot of office space, there is no guarantee that the rooms will always be occupied. And hotels, unlike offices, require expensive services like public rooms and laundry facilities which cost money and manpower to provide. By comparison, the overheads and running costs of offices are low and, once let, the tenants are likely to stay for some time. Given the fact that every square foot of Hong Kong is precious, and therefore must pay its way, it is understandable that Mr Li doesn't regard hotels as good business propositions—the rate of return simply isn't very good. He keeps the Hilton on, as he puts it, 'as a service to visitors like you. So that you will come and see our lovely city.'

Shortage of space is the crucial factor. As Trevor Bedford explains: 'The economy is almost totally land dominated. We have no resources, we have no coal, we have no North Sea Oil. All we've got is land.' And there isn't much—in all about four hundred square miles. The result has been a boom in land values. It doesn't seem to worry the government—it dovetails with their laissez-faire philosophy. The Financial Secretary, John Bremridge, sees the boom as inevitable:

> This is a small place; it's a successful place, it's a booming place—there's a great deal of money around. It is pretty obvious what will happen. If there's a short supply of anything and there's a lot of money about, the price will go up. That's what the market is all about.

In this case the results of the free operation of the market suit the government. Because of an accident of history, the biggest property speculator in Hong Kong is the government. In the early days of Hong Kong's history, the British government in London was reluctant to pay anything towards the costs of running the colony and insisted that the Hong Kong government should be financially self-supporting. In a letter to Sir Henry Pottinger, the governor of Hong Kong in 1843, Britain's Foreign Secretary, Lord Aberdeen, demonstrated a grasp of the economics of property speculation unusual in a nineteenth-century aristocrat:

> The principle source from which revenue is to be looked for is the land; and if, by the liberality of the commercial regulations enforced in the island, foreigners as well as British subjects are tempted to establish themselves on it, and thus to make it a great mercantile

The Property King

Like an amiable version of King Kong, Trevor Bedford takes buildings out of their place in his model of central Hong Kong and replaces
them with newer, bigger ones. 'Such lovely properties we've got,
really lovely stuff,' he says as he waves a negligent hand over a few
hundred million pounds worth of buildings. The chairman of Hong
Kong Land Corporation, the colony's richest property company, has
a beautifully constructed model of Hong Kong in his office which
shows all the main buildings of the central area of the city. It enables
Bedford to talk about his massive projects and illustrate them as he
talks. 'I think you could say pretty well that we control half of Hong
Kong and Victoria City. All the main high-rise buildings you see here
belong to us.' Ask Bedford which building he finds most attractive
and the answer comes quickly: 'My predecessor once said that the
only really attractive building was a fully let building.'

If Bedford sounds like an archetypal property tycoon, born and
bred in the mystique of plot ratios and site assembly, it is a misleading
impression. He was a Second Lieutenant in the Warwickshire Regiment in Korea, then spent six years in Shell as a management trainee.
He made an unusual move sideways into government, and worked as
a civil servant for four years in a variety of jobs—including the Hong
Kong government's anti-corruption squad—before returning to the
business world as boss of Hong Kong Land. The company is one of
the most venerable institutions of Hong Kong, dating back almost as
far as the colony itself. Its fortunes are closely tied to those of Hong
Kong. By judicious investment over the years, Hong Kong Land has
most of the prime sites. Just to remind you that the company owns
them, they are linked by overhead walkways.

Bedford is one of the new breed of Brits out East—not the old
colonial type at all. 'That type is dead, believe me. You've got to be
good to survive today in Hong Kong.' It is said with the confidence of
a true survivor.

Above: Sha Tin New Town; below: fire at a squatter village where 5,000 people were made homeless.

The Star ferry crossing the harbour.

Hong Kong Land Corporation advertisement showing how much of central Hong Kong they own.

entrepot . . . Her Majesty's Government conceives that they would be fully justified in securing to the Crown all the benefits to be expected from the increased value which such a state of things would confer upon the land. Her Majesty's government would therefore caution you against the permanent alienation of any portion of the land.

Sir Henry and his successors have followed this advice—to the enormous profit of the government, and therefore the taxpayers, of Hong Kong.

All land in Hong Kong is owned by the Crown and leased off for development. This means that the Hong Kong government is effectively a partner of the property developers. It has a vested interest in securing good prices for land. It also means that in one respect Hong Kong is a very socialist place, an irony that John Bremridge appreciates:

> In Hong Kong land policy is actually what successive Labour governments have tried to achieve in England for the lasty forty years without success. All profits, prime profits on land which is produced by government come back to the community.

One of the best spectator sports in the colony is the regular sales of prime patches of land. The auctioneer calls the prices out in English and his assistant repeats the figures in Chinese. The atmosphere is reminiscent of a Sotheby's or a Christie's sale. Prices are very high by the standards of the

55

rest of the world. One lot of industrial land in Kowloon, less than one-third of an acre in size, sold recently at auction for £2 million. In February 1982 a sensational property deal confirmed Hong Kong's reputation as the world leader in land prices. The government announced that it wished to sell a site next to the Connaught Centre. It was 144,000 square feet in size; or the equivalent of just over two football pitches. It was being used on only one level as a bus terminal—a shameful waste of space in a place as crowded as Hong Kong. The government put it up to sale by tender. In order to get the highest possible price for it, they gave it a special lot number—8668. The number eight is lucky for the Chinese, with connotations of prosperity; six sounds like the word for happiness. Thus the number given to the Connaught lot, roughly translated, means 'prosperity, double happiness, prosperity', a subtle appeal to Chinese superstitions about lucky numbers. Before the sale, Hong Kong Land's Trevor Bedford estimated the total cost of the project at over £1 billion sterling, after taking purchase and building costs into consideration. His company was particularly keen to get the site in order to strengthen its hold on the central business area of Hong Kong.

Bedford's bid for the site was accepted at four and three-quarter billion Hong Kong dollars—about £440 million. On that site Hong Kong Land plans to erect two towers, containing about 800,000 square feet of office space each, and a third smaller block of 500,000 square feet—making it, at 2.1 million square feet, one of the largest office developments in the world. Hong Kong Land should get its money back; even with a total outlay of £1 billion sterling, the complex will cost per square foot about the going market rate for offices in the centre of the city. That doesn't take into account the fact that property values are likely to be much higher by the time the buildings are ready for occupation. Inflation will make the Connaught deal a good investment.

The sale will provide almost 15 per cent of total government revenues for the coming year, which will benefit Hong Kong's taxpayers. Taxes are low in Hong Kong—the top tax rate is only 15 per cent and overall tax take on incomes is about half what it is in the United Kingdom—largely because of the profitable sideline in land dealing. It is estimated that overall 40 per cent of government revenue comes from land and land-related activities. There is a further benefit to government since much of what would otherwise be public expenditure on the rebuilding of infrastructure can be shifted off onto property companies as part of a land deal.

At the Connaught site, for example, Hong Kong Land will be required to rebuild the bus terminal on the ground floor of their new development. This will be done at the company's expense, thereby saving public money. In the offing is a property deal involving Kai Tak airport which will dwarf the Connaught project in size—and in the saving of public money. The airport is in the wrong place; it is on a slab of land stretching out into the harbour, and planes approaching from inland have to come in low over Kowloon, making a sharp turn about twenty seconds before landing. The result is that the bottom of the Kowloon peninsular is a rather dirty and noisy place. It is also a part of town that is not heavily built

The most expensive bus station in the world.

up; there is a height restriction—imposed by the safety requirements of the airport—of about fifteen stories—the equivalent of about two hundred feet. Plans are being considered to move the airport out of town. Either it will be put on the nearly deserted island of Lan Tau, which will then be linked to the main area of Hong Kong by a bridge, or, more ambitiously, it will be rebuilt in the border region. As a New Territories airport it could then serve not only Hong Kong but also China. In one optimistic version of the border airport, the actual runways will run from Hong Kong into China, thereby making the new airport a genuinely international one.

The economic benefits to government would be immense. Releasing the land at Kai Tak for redevelopment as industrial space or housing, and removing the height restriction on buildings in the Kowloon peninsular would produce a bonanza for the government's land account. Government officials estimate that redevelopment profits from selling off this land could pay for the entire cost of the new airport, wherever it is built.

Such massive government involvement in property speculation is already being used elsewhere to the benefit of the community. The new Mass Transit Railway, which links central Hong Kong to the suburbs of Kowloon, is financing itself by judicious property speculation. The costs of engineering such a massive system are so high, and the fares so low, that it could never pay for itself on conventional accounting methods. Since the government is reluctant to subsidise public transport, sites above the various stations of the MTR are being sold off to developers for large sums.

These sites are known in the developers' jargon as 'airspace'—the right to build above an existing edifice.

There is a less attractive side to government involvement in property speculation. With so much revenue at stake, the government is reluctant to stand in the way of any redevelopment scheme, regardless of what it entails. A recent example is the demolition of the Repulse Bay Hotel. This beautiful piece of British colonial architecture was one of the few remaining landmarks of old Hong Kong, but as a low-rise building, it was something of an anachronism. It has now been pulled down so that the site can be used for multi-storey luxury apartment blocks. The hotel was already surrounded by apartment blocks, and few in Hong Kong believe it could have been saved. The colony's few conservationists fought a rearguard action—not only against the developers but also government, which knew it would get a slice of the profits from the hotel's demolition. Critics argue that Hong Kong lacks any concept of planning for the public interest. The government cannot be an arbiter when it is also a participant, and there have been frequent examples of bad planning decisions which came about because of the pressure to maximise profit to government.

As Hong Kong becomes an increasingly complex and affluent society, the need for careful planning of the resource in shortest supply, land, is becoming more and more evident. The government is trying to ease the strains on land by a typically large-scale Hong Kong solution. It is an axiom in the property business that the best thing about land is that they aren't making it any more. In Hong Kong they are. Alarmed at the pressures of demand on land, the government has taken steps to increase its supply. Most of the colony is mountainous and there is very little flat land; the solution has been to chop the tops off mountains and push the land out into the sea. That process has been going on for a long time; the seafront of modern Hong Kong is about a quarter of a mile further out into the harbour than it was when the island was first taken by Britain. But in recent years the process of creating land has speeded up. Tsing Yi used to be a quiet and remote island, off the west coast of the Kowloon peninsular, peopled by peasants living in primitive conditions. It is no longer an island but is now part of the mainland, joined up by large-scale reclamation. The new city of Sha Tin in the New Territories is another case: ten years ago, it was a quiet inlet inhabited by a few thousand peasant farmers and fishermen. Most of the inlet has been filled in and today the original population are living in the middle of an inland city, as opposed to the coastal village where they grew up.

It is one of the ironies of Hong Kong that if China renews the lease in 1997 they will be getting back more than was leased in the first place. The equivalent of the City of Westminster—the whole West End of London—has been added to Hong Kong's land area. But, although enormous efforts have been made in recent years to increase the supply of land, there is a limit to the amount which can be manufactured; it is not enough to meet demand which inevitably means that the upward spiral of prices will continue.

The impact of these rising land prices on the economy as a whole is a further cause for concern. Observers detect a reluctance on the part of

Peasant children in a New Territories village—as landowners, they are potential millionaires.

government to take any action which might harm the interests of the property men. Journalist Philip Bowring sees it as the inevitable result of an unholy alliance between business and government:

> I don't think they are aware of this being a conspiracy, it is just a feeling of general mutual interest. The tremendous expansion of credit, at a rate of about 50 per cent increase in two years, is an example. This is obviously highly inflationary; it has created a property boom which has also led to a stock market boom. Now to stop that boom you've got to apply some sort of pressure on the banking system. But the banks are under pressure from the property companies who have got themselves into the position where they need constant injections of cheap money, like a drug. So the government, although it keeps saying this is bad for Hong Kong, does nothing about it. It therefore puts the interests of the majority of people, who want a lower rate of inflation, behind this desire to give easy money to the developers.

Hong Kong's inflation rate in 1981 was officially estimated at 15 per cent, but many believe this is an underestimate. Government does not seem unduly worried by this figure, preferring to leave corrective measures to the marketplace. The philosophy of laissez-faire means that even if government wanted to intervene, it is not in a position to do so.

Monetary controls are almost non-existent. Most finance ministers have a battery of weapons to fight inflation. Hong Kong has none of these. There is no exchange control, which means the money supply can expand—and contract—unchecked by government. The government runs at a profit, largely because of its land policy, and therefore cannot influence interest rates by its need to borrow money. Financial Secretary, John Bremridge, argues that Hong Kong's problem

> is the problem of success. We have too much money around . . . and that had a very inflationary effect because so many of the banks were lending unwisely, and not as good prudent bankers, to speculators. But as always happens in Hong Kong one had a degree of confidence that as long as government didn't meddle, it would tend to sort itself out.

It did in fact sort itself out on that occasion and the property boom slowed down, although inflation still remains high. There was relief that the market did work in this case. One consequence of Hong Kong's success at attracting foreign bankers to the colony has been that the informal gentleman's agreement, which used to regulate matters, no longer applies. In the past, when banking was dominated by the Hong Kong and Shanghai Bank and a handful of others, a simple phone call from the financial secretary would have resulted in a gentle brake being applied to lending. Today, with hundreds of banks competing vigorously in Hong Kong's cut-throat money market, gentlemanly tactics aren't guaranteed to succeed. When Mr Bremridge used such tactics in the autumn of 1981, he eventually persuaded the banks to raise interest rates. But it was done, as he puts it, 'not without a certain amount of sucking of teeth'. He admits that the economy could easily have got out of hand: 'There's always a risk in a free economy of balloons blowing up and bursting. I think you've seen the market acting to stop this happening. It has worked actually . . . thank goodness.'

Critics agree that more positive measures of control are needed. Although property prices in Hong Kong have eased in the wake of the world recession, no one doubts that they could shoot through the roof again. The factor that would precipitate government action would be a reluctance on the part of big multi-nationals to set up a base in Hong Kong because office accommodation was too expensive—already office space in the central district is the most expensive in the world. At the moment there is no sign of any reluctance to pay Hong Kong rents; other factors make Hong Kong too attractive a location. But if there were to be another property boom next year, which forced rents much higher, foreign companies would think twice about investing in Hong Kong. Next time round, the informal controls and gentle chivvying that worked in 1981 might not be so successful.

An additional complication in this property game is that there is a new player on the board. Over the last few years, the People's Republic of China has been putting money into Hong Kong's booming property market. It seems strange that China, which does not recognise the validity of the British lease of Hong Kong, should buy back what it believes it already

Driving Out the Evil Spirits

To the most casual passer-by, something is wrong about the two huge bronze lions outside the offices of the Hong Kong and Shanghai Banking Corporation in central Hong Kong. They're not square on to each other, and you'd think that a well-run company like the bank would make sure they got that right. The reason for the asymmetrical lions is that it would have been bad 'fung shui' to place them in direct alignment. 'Fung shui' is essentially the Chinese way of assuring prosperity and good fortune—in this case the correct alignment of objects so that the maximum amount of good fortune will come from a building or office. Even in a place as sophisticated as Hong Kong, it isn't wise to ignore the fung shui man. When the bank moved its headquarters, and with it the famous lions, the fung shui man was brought in to advise on the most propitious siting for the statues outside the new office. Even Western bankers whose business has more to do with balance sheets than black magic cannot ignore Chinese custom.

Go into any leading Chinese businessman's office and you may feel that it could have been more conveniently arranged. But don't touch anything. It's a sure bet that the positioning was on the advice of the fung shui man.

The essential principle of fung shui is that it is very unlucky if the arrangement of objects allows the prosperous winds that enter a building or a room to blow straight out the other side. Thus, while a Western architect for convenience and neatness' sake might put two doors in a room opposite each other, a Chinese architect would try and avoid that.

Those who ignore fung shui do so at their peril. The mammoth Connaught Centre on the waterfront in Hong Kong allegedly has bad fung shui and, as a result, many Chinese are reluctant to go in there. A friend with an office in the building told me he had taken great trouble to align all the office furniture in such a way as to counteract the bad fung shui of the building as a whole. The building—which has hundreds of round windows in it—is known unkindly to superstitious and hostile Chinese as 'the building of a thousand arseholes'. Not a flattering description for the biggest skyscraper in Hong Kong, but that is the price of bad fung shui.

owns. The amounts involved are large, though no one knows quite how large because of the Chinese habit of investing jointly with local companies. One merchant bank in Hong Kong concluded that China had invested at least £300 million and possibly as much as £1 billion sterling in property in the colony. The Bank of China building, in the central district, is believed to be worth something like £80 million, a value which will rise steadily with inflation.

Hong Kong has taken this Chinese investment in its property boom as a sign that the People's Republic has no hostile intentions towards the colony. This has been a contributory factor in boosting the confidence of the property market. The government has fallen over backwards to assist Peking in this venture: a process that, according to some critics, has exacerbated the very problems that government, in its other role as a regulator of the market, has been trying to solve. As Philip Bowring comments:

> You have seen instances where People's Republic of China corporations have been getting grants of land at outrageously cheap prices. It seems to me ridiculous that government here is caving in to the specific demands and interests of people across the border.

Bowring believes that the position of Chinese banks in Hong Kong is also causing problems:

> In the financial sector the Bank of China has been one of the leaders in this splurge of credit. The administration is not gutsy at the best of times, but now you have the situation here where if anybody in Peking says jump, they do tend to jump.

If the property business has been the making of Hong Kong, it is now in danger of becoming the cross on the colony's back. With high inflation damaging Hong Kong's ability to compete in the world's markets, and massive fortunes to be made at home from property speculation, Hong Kong's industrial base could be undermined from within. Hong Kong is still primarily a manufacturing economy—and the cure for runaway inflation caused by property speculation would be tough financial measures that could do the manufacturing sector untold harm. Increased government intervention seems inevitable, if only to protect the interests of its new Chinese partners. But that will depend on whether the government can steel its nerve to a role that is unfamiliar and demanding. Philip Bowring doesn't think it can:

> You've got a situation here where you actually need more government, not less; and a government which can stand up to pressures, whether from local pressure groups, or Peking or London. That's what we haven't got.

CHAPTER SIX

THE WHITE MAN'S BURDEN

No honours were bestowed on the first British official responsible for the administration of Hong Kong. Captain Charles Elliot RN, Her Majesty's Superintendent of Trade for China, and effectively the colony's first administrator, was also the man who exacted Hong Kong from China after the First Opium War. For this he was roundly ticked off by Lord Palmerston:

> You have disobeyed and neglected your instructions; you have deliberately abstained from employing the force placed at your disposal; and you have, without sufficient necessity, accepted terms which fall far short of those you were instructed to obtain.

The unfortunate captain was dismissed and sent even further into exile, first to Texas as consul-general, then to St Helena as governor.

Since Elliot's day, the British administrators of Hong Kong have continued to suffer from the feeling of being unwanted in London. The masters of Hong Kong have also been regarded warily by their subjects, whose view of their British masters is at best indifferent, at worst hostile. As a result, the weight of 'the white man's burden' has seemed to lie heavily on the shoulders of Hong Kong's rulers, who feel increasingly uncomfortable about the outmoded system of colonial government. They are the last relics of an imperial age, increasingly out of step in the modern world.

Sir Alexander Grantham, Governor of Hong Kong from 1947 to 1957, found the awe which surrounded a colonial governor uncomfortable:

> The governor is next to the Almighty. Everyone stands up when he enters the room. He is deferred to on all occasions. It is always 'Yes Sir', 'Certainly Your Excellency'. It is good for a governor when on leave to take his place in the queue and to have his toes trodden on in a crowded railway carriage. It brings home to him that he is but an ordinary mortal like everyone else, and that the dignity attaches to the office and not the individual.

Grantham's attitude was shared by His Excellency Sir Crawford Murray MacLehose GBE, KCMG, KCVO, Governor of Hong Kong for eleven years until his retirement in May 1982. At 6' 6", he towered over almost

everyone in Hong Kong. In other respects he was careful not to tower. Some critics complain that he caught the traditional governor's disease of arrogance—'they all think they can cross Hong Kong harbour without waiting for the ferry'—but Sir Murray was a long way from the normal image of a British colonial governor. He hated putting on his full governor's uniform (a cocked hat with white feathers, a button-up white drill jacket and white trousers) and only did for the formal state occasions. In part this was due to his aversion to the petty trappings of imperialism and pomp. Cynical civil servants, with long memories going back to the early days of Sir Murray's rule, claim there was another reason. Apparently on a particularly hot day, while he was in full dress uniform, the heat melted the wax which holds the ostrich feathers in the cocked hat, and they started drooping in a most undignified fashion.

Though he wore a normal business suit for everyday work and social functions, Sir Murray was often to be seen in slacks and an open shirt, diving enthusiastically round one of the government's housing projects, in which he had a special interest. Though he was one of the last and certainly the most important of Britain's remaining colonial governors, Sir Murray did not come up via the Colonial Office route of his predecessors. Unlike them, his background was in the diplomatic service. A China expert, he had run the Foreign Office's Far East desk for a couple of years, as well as having been a consular official in Hankow during the 1949 Chinese revolution. It was a sign of the times that a diplomat and not a colonial office man should

Sir Murray MacLehose in the governor's uniform he didn't like wearing.

have been appointed to Hong Kong. It was widely viewed at the time as a political tactic aimed at pleasing the Chinese government.

Any early thoughts that Sir Murray might be a good diplomat and little else have been removed by his performance as governor. In his eleven years he has been a tremendous success both as diplomat and as an administrator, with few blots on his record. He has won widespread admiration on all sides for his ability to run the machinery of government; indeed, some Chinese wondered at his retiring so early; in relation to the average age of China's leaders, sixty-five is considered comparatively young.

In theory the governor is the last of the autocrats, absolute ruler over five and a half million people. In practice, as Sir Murray acknowledges, pragmatism dictates otherwise:

> I remember how someone who was visiting from another country put it to me once. He said, 'I can do this'—referring to some particularly high-handed action—'because I'm the Prime Minister of a young democracy. You can't because you're an old-fashioned dictator.' There's a lot of truth in that. Because we have a somewhat anachronistic form of government, we have to be very careful.

Sir Murray has certainly been careful—no doubt helped by his experience as a diplomat. Initially, however, his foreign office background was not a great deal of help:'It is an extraordinary experience going from what I would call the co-pilot's seat to the pilot's seat. Quite different.'

The particular plane that Sir Murray was called on to fly was a sort of administrative version of a DC3—ancient in construction and design, but robust and still in quite sound working order. The colonial structure means that the governor is appointed from Whitehall; in theory by the Queen in council—in practice that means by the Foreign and Commonwealth Office, which has absorbed the old Colonial Office. Hong Kong does have a constitution of sorts: it was written in 1917 though various amendments have been added since. The Letters Patent and Royal Instructions to the Governor of Hong Kong, which act as the constitution, are magisterially vague documents: 'We do hereby authorise, empower and command Our said Governor and Commander-in-Chief to do and execute all things that belong to his said office . . . according to such instructions as may from time to time be given to him'. There follows a list of do's and don't's which are phrased in the broadest possible terms. Like many British constitutional documents, the Royal Instructions are permissive in tone, aimed at leaving as much as possible to the good sense of the man on the spot. The governor has in theory almost unlimited power. Under the heading 'Emergencies' the instructions state: 'On any occasion which the Governor in Council may consider to be an occasion of emergency or public danger he may make any regulations whatsoever he may consider desirable in the public interest.' These can override the normal rule of law if required. There can be few constitutions today which grant such a degree of formal latitude to the ruler.

To assist him in the execution of his duties, the governor has a cabinet, called the Executive Council or Exco, which has sixteen members. Seven of them are civil servants, the so-called 'official' members—the Governor, the Chief Secretary (roughly equivalent to Britain's head of the Civil Service), the Commander of British Forces, the Financial Secretary, the Attorney General, the Secretary of Home Affairs and the Secretary for the New Territories. They are outnumbered by what are known, rather quaintly, as the 'unofficials'—outsiders appointed by the governor to help in the running of government. There are nine of them: they currently include a Catholic priest, the chief executive of Jardine Matheson, oldest of the trading companies, the chairman of the Hong Kong and Shanghai Bank (the government's banker), a hospital consultant and a clutch of influential Chinese businessmen. It must be the most extraordinary composition for a cabinet anywhere in the world. But in a curious way it seems to work.

The Governor in Council is legally the Government of Hong Kong—through the council the governor enacts legislation and ordinances, makes regulations and hears appeals. In theory the governor is only advised by his council: it is he who decides what should appear on the agenda. He can ignore the advice given to him by Exco and isn't bound by anything Exco says or does without his consent. In practice, no governor can ever exercise his despotic powers. Sir Murray's reign has been dominated by the search for some form of implied consent which can give legitimacy to colonial government.

Hong Kong is ruled by what government supporters term consensus, and by what their critics see as following the line of least resistance. The consensus theory was defined in 1975 by the Secretary of Home Affairs, Denis Bray. Government proceeds, he said,

> by consensus rather than debate, for this is the only course open to a government required to continue indefinitely in power. Consensus implies consultation, negotiation and compromise on a scale that would be unacceptable to a party returned to power at an election.

This process of compromise is enhanced by a further consultative body, the Legislative Council. This council is also known by its shorthand title of Legco and, like Exco, consists of a number of officials and unofficials. There are fifty-four members (the numbers increase from time to time), half of whom are civil servants, the other half unofficial government appointees. It is presided over by the governor and meets once a fortnight throughout the year with a break during the summer. Its deliberations take place in an ugly chunk of municipal architecture tacked on to the end of the government's main offices half-way up the hill above central Hong Kong. The impression of municipality is strengthened by watching its proceedings. The standard of debate is appalling. No one interrupts and the long set-piece speeches are delivered in monotones without an ounce of oratory or feeling. To a visitor it looks more like the annual general meeting of an obscure insurance company than the parliament of a flourishing and lively city state. The public is allowed in, but there is never a queue.

Legco is an ersatz parliament, but it does perform a useful function as

The New Mandarin

'I've never pretended in government to find the right answers. All I try and do is be less wrong.' Scarcely a statement you would expect to hear from a government minister, but it's a typically deprecating self-assessment from Hong Kong's Financial Secretary, John Bremridge. He is a classic Hong Kong type, who has drifted from private business into government via the mass of consultative committees which run Hong Kong. He was one of the great 'taipans'—Chairman and Chief Executive of one of the mighty Hongs, the Swire Group, which owns, among other companies, one of the world's most profitable airlines, Cathay Pacific. When he decided to work for the government and accepted the post of Financial Secretary, there was astonishment in government and business circles. Business critics argued that he was a 'second-rate businessman' in the old colonial mould. Government officials were worried by his pragmatic approach and his lack of knowledge of the theory of economics—he has a second-class degree in jurisprudence.

Opinions have changed. John Bremridge's pragmatism is now seen as a great strength. He sees his role as the unflappable captain on the bridge, occasionally altering direction, but essentially hoping that the good sense of the crew will keep the ship on course. 'I think it's very dangerous for economists and even worse for pseudo-economists like me to try and foretell the future, because you really can't tell what's going to happen.' It's a modest self-assessment, but given the terrible disasters that have befallen finance ministers with much greater ambitions, it is a reasonable one.

All I say is that our policy is to let market forces decide. When market forces can't decide, then we accept we have to intervene. But I won't intervene where it won't work . . . I've never believed in the theory of blacks and whites. All the time you're choosing a shade of grey. There are very few clear-cut solutions. Let time be the healer.

a watchdog over the work of government. Much of its most useful work is as ombudsman, chasing up complaints of individuals against the administration. Its unofficial members are appointed by government, but that doesn't necessarily make them government yes-men. As Roger Lobo, a businessman who is leader of the unofficials, points out, not being elected can have its advantages:

> We don't have parties as you do in England, and therefore we don't have to toe the party line regardless of conscience and beliefs. We vote or go along with what we believe is right for the people, what's right for Hong Kong, and what's right for our consciences.

The knowledge of their non-elected status makes unofficials highly sensitive to public opinion: as Lydia Dunn, another unofficial, notes: 'You could argue that we are more sensitive to public opinion than, say, a normal elected member would be.' The essence of the system, she feels, is that unofficials feel responsible to the community as a whole rather than to sectional interests: 'Are sectional interests always the best for the community? This is where I think our system has worked. My colleagues always think in terms of what is best for Hong Kong as a whole.'

As a system of government it seems to work, perhaps because ideology is not a political issue in Hong Kong as it is in most other places. Everyone is agreed on the need for government to limit its role—or as the Chief Secretary to the Government, Sir Philip Haddon-Cave, puts it: 'A government which attempts more than it ought will perform less.' The issues which convulse political life elsewhere are missing in Hong Kong. Those that do arise are of an administrative nature—unfairness to an individual or a small group by a department of government. For such cases, Legco is ideal. Government listens: it would be a rash governor who ignored the feelings of Legco. For the community Legco is a useful sounding board; for government it is a valuable storm-warning system.

Undoubtedly, there are real limitations. The non-elected nature of Legco means that it offers no real sense of representation or participation in government for the people of Hong Kong. Those chosen to serve on Legco come from a very limited stratum of society: they are usually from the business world, and the top of the business world at that. In no way can they be said to represent the attitudes and aspirations of the ordinary working-class family in Kowloon.

There are other drawbacks to this system of government by consensus. Its critics claim that consensus really means doing whatever is easiest. Precisely because government is so unrepresentative—a small number of British administrators, representing less than 2 per cent of the population, ruling the 98 per cent who are Chinese—it leans over backwards to accommodate opposition. Journalist Philip Bowring disputes that the system works in the best interests of the whole community:

> What you have here is a bunch of pressure groups each pushing their own particular barrow and trying to get the government to do what is

The arms of Hong Kong—the lion and the dragon.

best for them. The government is very sensitive to the fact that it is unrepresentative, so that anyone coming along and saying they represent the interests of the masses is listened to.

Sir Murray MacLehose sees the force of the argument: 'You say pressure group, I say public opinion. But, yes, we are more sensitive to public opinion, pressure groups, than an elected government would be. You've got to govern by consent.'

The normal route for a British Crown Colony like Hong Kong would be a gradual progression towards representative elected government. That route is not open to Hong Kong, not because Britain opposes it, but because China has intimated that it would not tolerate the creation of an independent state on Chinese soil. China regards Hong Kong as an inalienable part of its territory: the introduction of democracy, which might in turn lead to aspirations for independence from Britain and China, would be unacceptable. It is a view echoed by senior government officials, who believe they are running Hong Kong on behalf of China, as trustees for the future. Financial Secretary, John Bremridge, disputes that Hong Kong is even a colony in the old sense of the word: 'This place is a pseudo colony. I think that Lord Kadoorie got this place right when he said some years ago that Hong Kong is now the free trade zone of China under British management.'

Nonetheless British officials are uneasy about their theoretically unrestrained power and have gone to great lengths to try and give it some

69

legitimacy. They have begun to move tentatively towards democracy— though only so far as can be guaranteed not to offend Peking. Half the members of the Urban Council are now elected; the other half are still appointed by government. This is scarcely a breakthrough for democratic accountability but it is a start. The Urban Council controls less than 4 per cent of government spending, and its power extends over such minor issues as museum management, garbage disposal and the licensing of hawkers. The government has decided to extend the experiment to the administration of the New Territories. The aim is to provide, as a government spokesman cautiously put it, 'an expanded opportunity for public participation in administration'. The issues entrusted to the democratically elected members are still small fry. At one of its recent meetings the district board for Sha Tin new town spent over an hour on lengthy discussion of the wording and design for a sign saying 'Welcome to Sha Tin'.

The government's obsession with introducing some accountability is undermined by the general lack of enthusiasm for democracy. Turnout at elections is low, although officials were delighted at a much better than expected figure for the New Territories District Board elections, held in March 1982. The Chinese, by and large, want to get on with their own affairs without interference from government. As John Walden, formerly a senior civil servant with responsibility for keeping tabs on Chinese opinion, explains:

> It's not the nature of this sort of society to confront; people much prefer to deal with problems behind the scenes rather than all get together and yell for what they want. I don't think the Chinese want to get involved; they just want good government. They just want to make sure there's someone keeping an eye on what the government is doing.

In addition to the limited steps towards some form of democratic accountability, the government uses an extraordinary network of consultative committees to help it to keep in touch with the governed. There are currently well over three hundred and more are spawned by the week. John Walden, who was charged with monitoring this exercise in quangoism, found that many civil servants disliked this level of consultation. He made himself unpopular with his colleagues when he reported in 1980, that 'One finds, regrettably, dedicated civil servants who still regard public consultation as a troublesome and time-wasting impediment to their well-laid plans for solving Hong Kong's problems.' Nor was the problem all one sided. Walden also found there were 'Too many unofficial committee members who, while relishing the prestige associated with appointment to important consultative committees, never expressed a dissenting view for fear of compromising the usefulness of close proximity to influential government officials.'

Walden believes that the relationship of governors and governed has improved: 'I think the government now knows what's happening all right, although I am not sure the people know what the government is doing.'

Like many civil servants who were in Hong Kong during the 1960s, Walden is haunted by the memory of the riots which shook the stability and self-confidence of the British rulers. Trouble was sparked off in 1966 by a proposal for a small increase in the fares on the Star ferry across the harbour. Protests against this led to violent rioting—a reaction out of all proportion to the problem. The incident terrified the government; to this day fares on the Star ferry have been kept artificially low. With a first-class fare across the harbour costing about 7 pence, it must be the best value for money of any transport system in the world. Although the official view is that the communications gap between government and people has been bridged, the government's nightmare is that it could get tripped up again by a similar issue.

The 1966 riots did little for the government's self-confidence. It is constantly on the alert, watching that it does not give offence—even on the smaller issues. The word colony, for example, is the accurate technical description of Hong Kong and its administration, yet it never passes the lips of a civil servant in Hong Kong. It is taboo. Hong Kong is always referred to as a 'territory' or an 'entity'. Sir Murray MacLehose sighs deeply when asked about the ban:

> Well, colony is a dirty word, I suppose as a result of United Nations criticism. It seems somehow or other to suggest people digging desperately in an alien soil, and Hong Kong isn't like that at all. It is a great big cosmopolitan city. I'm sure Marx would have a fit if he saw Hong Kong.

But watching Sir Murray during one of his rare appearances as governor in full dress uniform—the laying of wreaths on Armistice Sunday—the notion of the British as toilers in an alien soil comes across powerfully. The trappings of pomp, the ritual of the two-minute silence, the lone bugler playing the last post—all this is redolent of a way of life that is completely alien to Hong Kong. The Chinese watching seemed to find it a curious ceremony. Looking at the crowd, one wondered if the deaths of British soldiers in a European World War more than sixty years ago means anything to Chinese onlookers.

The Hong Kong government is not helped in its search for legitimacy by the British connection. At times it seems as if Britain is more of a millstone round Hong Kong's neck than its supporter and friend. There is a widespread—but erroneous—notion that Hong Kong's large foreign currency reserves are used to prop up sterling's exchange rate, to the detriment of the best interests of Hong Kong. British interest in the political affairs of the colony is sporadic. Whitehall rarely intervenes, preferring to leave policy decisions to the Hong Kong government. Occasional parliamentary delegations from Britain are a worse offender. In a lightning tour round the sights, MPs are inclined to lecture Hong Kong on the evils of their highly effective textile exports, or berate government for not being more democratic. Such visitors are unwelcome in Hong Kong.

Relations between colony and mother country are cool at best— Britain is viewed a bit like a music hall mother-in-law: a sort of meddlesome

Armistice Day wreath-laying ceremony.

nuisance, given to sudden interference and nagging. Recently several issues have widened the gap. Britain's seeming reluctance to protect Hong Kong's interests in the Multi Fibre Arrangement negotiations, the raising of fees for overseas students and the Nationality Act, which deprived Hong Kongers of a proper passport and confirmed that they have no rights to settle in Britain, are all issues which have confirmed the belief that Britain cares little for Hong Kong. As Dr Gordon Redding of Hong Kong University says:

> We have a few friends in London, but we have an awful lot of enemies in the businesses of Britain. You can't expect the British public to be terribly concerned about a colony a long way away which is doing very nicely thank you.

It is a view that has received some support from a recent incident: the protracted search for a new governor to replace Sir Murray MacLehose.

The issue attracted intense interest in Hong Kong. Endless columns of print were filled with lists of potential candidates. The *Far Eastern Economic Review* went so far as to print a fake advertisement for the post: 'Sit Vac. Good Pay. Pension after 1997.' In Britain there was almost no interest in the subject, despite the fact that some very well-known names were in the running for a plum job that commands a take-home pay much higher than that of the Prime Minister of Britain. 'Replacing Sir Murray as governor took months and months,' comments *Review* journalist, Philip

Nelson's Heirs

Outside the headquarters of the Captain-in-Charge, Hong Kong, a red bicycle leans against the wall. In rough white letters on its back mudguard reads the legend 'First Lieutenant'. It is an economical solution to the first lieutenant's problem of getting round the naval base, *HMS Tamar*—one that is hardly needed today since you can walk round the base in minutes. *HMS Tamar* is much reduced from the days of its glory, when it was home base to the once impressive China Squadron, with a full admiral in charge. The cruisers and the aircraft carriers have gone, and all that is left of the far-flung battle line of empire is a squadron of five ageing Ton-class patrol boats, which are beginning to show their age (they are mostly over twenty-five years old) and are scheduled to be replaced in the near future. Watching them come into harbour, one is conscious of seeing the last remnants of an imperial navy: crews are a mixture of European officers and some key ratings, and locally enlisted Chinese seamen. They are also the only ships in the Royal Navy to continue the old tradition of a ship's dog. Rabies' scares have driven other Navy dogs ashore, but the Hong Kong squadron never visits foreign ports and can therefore keep its mascots on board.

Most of the navy's time is spent chasing illegal immigrants, but with a top speed of fifteen knots, the elderly patrol boats can easily be outrun by a modern powerboat. They are a pretty sight nonetheless, chugging purposefully through the harbour and emphasise the fairy tale quality of Britain's military presence in Hong Kong. Like their colleagues in the army, navy men here know they will never be called on to fight—defence plans assume the colony is indefensible—but the sub-tropical climate and scenic waters of Hong Kong make it a popular posting and it also provides some useful experience in small ships. Given the fact that Hong Kong pays three-quarters of its defence costs, it is also a good bargain for Britain.

P1096

Bowring; 'No one in London of any stature seemed interested in the job. But being the governor of Hong Kong is a wonderful opportunity—direct personal authority over five million people. Incredible that no one should want it.'

A new governor has finally been appointed: the Under Secretary of State at the Foreign Office, Sir Edward Youde. He acknowledges the size of the job and the problem of filling Sir Murray's shoes—'It will be a hard act to follow.' In some respects Youde is well equipped for the job. He is a very senior Foreign Office man, with extensive knowledge of China. He has served there four times, once during the famous *Amethyst* incident when the frigate escaped from the Yangtze River, and has been Ambassador to China. He speaks fluent Mandarin Chinese—not that it will be much use in Hong Kong, where the majority of the population speak Cantonese—but it is a talent which certainly shows him to be a man with a real understanding of China and Chinese thinking. His appointment has been greeted with some enthusiasm in Peking, which is important because relations with Peking will dominate Sir Edward's governorship even more than they did Sir Murray's.

Keeping China sweet, even if it is the most important part of a governor's job, is not all that counts. Running Hong Kong has become an enormously complex exercise, calling for considerable administrative skills. The government has 140,000 employees and spends £2.5 billion sterling a year. Sir Edward has to avoid courting the criticism made of his predecessor—that Sir Murray's response to any problem was to throw money at it. Social

74

programmes have proliferated without much rhyme or reason, and no one is quite sure what the government is trying to achieve. Deciding what is essential and what is not, and how large a role government should play, poses a major problem. The faltering housing programme, a pet project of Sir Murray's, requires skilful handling. Sir Edward was reported to have taken a crash course in the subject before setting out for Hong Kong.

Perhaps the overriding problem facing Sir Edward is not relations with China or managing the burgeoning bureaucracy, but the rather more intangible one that lies behind both of those. As one British expatriate civil servant put it: 'Why are we here? We're here because we're here. That's why we're here.' Defining Britain's role in Hong Kong is the key to the success or failure of his term of office. At the moment the administration lacks a *raison d'être*. Philip Bowring sees this as the major flaw in British rule over Hong Kong:

> The colonial system is an anachronism, yet here it has to carry on. I think the administration faces a problem of identifying what it is supposed to be doing. So it carries on, but without any great feeling of its own self-assurance. No one is quite sure where paternalism ends and where serving the people begins. The government is always looking round nervously at what people are saying.

On the surface, Sir Murray MacLehose's period as governor has been a great success. Major crises have been weathered, the economic miracle has been sustained, and the past eleven years have seen an enormous improvement in the standard of living of ordinary Hong Kongers. But that economic success is now creating its own problems: how can government continue to meet the aspirations of Hong Kongers? How can the miracles of the last decade be repeated? Sir Edward Youde comes to Hong Kong with a reputation for careful attention to detail and an insistence on high standards of personal conduct and discipline—he is reported as having banned gambling among his colleagues in the Peking Embassy. But can he provide the necessary imaginative leap that will provide British government of Hong Kong with a reason to continue? Sir Murray, in a message to his successor, summed up the strengths—and weaknesses—of British rule:

> You'd expect me to tell him some subtle method of dealing with the future of Hong Kong, or to dealing with Whitehall. I don't think that's what would be in my mind at all. I would warn him against the dangers of isolation in Government House. This is a constant problem any governor has to face. In spite of having to spend most of his time here, in surroundings which aren't exactly conducive to free speech and informal advice, he's got to keep in contact with all shades of opinion in Hong Kong. So long as you're in contact with the people, you won't go far wrong.

It remains to be seen whether Sir Edward will take the advice of his predecessor.

CHAPTER SEVEN

A NEW JERUSALEM?

> Positive non-intervention involves taking the view that, in the great majority of circumstances, it is futile and damaging to the growth rate of the economy for attempts to be made to plan the allocation of resources available to the private sector and frustrate the operation of market forces.

That was how former Financial Secretary, Sir Philip Haddon-Cave, summed up the government's economic policy of laissez-faire. Sir Philip explained what this meant in relation to the government's other policies: 'As regards the dynamic without which individualism would be ineffectual, namely the work ethic, we take care that it is not eroded by social policies and redistributive fiscal policies.' Bold words these, guaranteed to raise a cheer from right-wing free-market economists, but which have become increasingly irrelevant in the context of a complex modern world. Hong Kong's government has found—in its social policies, as in its economic and financial policies—that the rigid rule of 'hands off' simply doesn't work.

For years it has been the proud boast of the government in Hong Kong that it does not cost its citizens much. Land sales have boosted government revenues, thereby lightening the taxpayer's burden, but government has also been cheap because it has done very little for those it governs. Social provisions have been meagre and, to be fair to government, that has been politically acceptable until recent times. The extent of the change in this attitude can be seen by looking at the proportion of the Gross Domestic Product consumed by government. In the 1950s it was among the lowest in the world at 11 per cent; by the end of the 1960s it had risen to 13 per cent, by the end of the 1970s to 19 per cent; today it is about 24 per cent. In other words, government spends one in every four dollars in Hong Kong. It is still far behind Britain and similar countries with a full-blown welfare state, but the rate of increase is very rapid and shows no signs of slackening.

The government of Hong Kong has woken up to the age of the welfare state. It has found that it has to create and sustain an infrastructure; it has also found that building such an infrastructure is expensive and maintaining it is a continuing drain on the public purse. In 1981/2 the government spent £1.5 billion on a variety of social programmes, something like three-fifths of government's total expenditure. It is an upward curve: over the last three years expenditure on roads, civil engineering, housing, education, ameni-

ties and social welfare has doubled. Anywhere else such a phenomenon would be regarded as a step in the right direction; in Hong Kong there is worry that such largesse might undermine the work ethic.

The growth of the welfare state has dented the rigid 'hands off' philosophy of government. Philosophically it is explained as sorting out the inevitable distortions of the marketplace. Financial Secretary, John Bremridge, thinks it has led to the burial of the laissez-faire attitude of government:

> There is a widespread canard that the government of Hong Kong is a laissez-faire government, which is totally false. People don't seem to realise that as a government we now house 45 per cent of the population; we have the biggest public housing scheme in the world here. By the mid 1980s we shall be housing 60 per cent of the population. This is certainly not the mark of non-intervention. It's a clear sign that we intervene when we have to and when the market forces can't cope.

The history of Hong Kong's massive public housing programme, which already caters for about two million people, is a good example of how government pragmatism has reacted to some inevitable geographical logic. There is no housing market in Hong Kong except for the super-rich and the very poor. There are only a few hundred houses on Hong Kong island—

land there is much too expensive to build just one- or two-floor buildings. Owning a house on the island is a sure sign that you are a multi-millionaire. At the other end of the scale, the newly arrived immigrants live in whatever they can afford: on the road out to Tuen Mun there is a container by the side of the road. Crude windows and a door have been hacked out with a blow torch and it is home to a family. Between these two extremes housing is subsidised or controlled in some way. At the bottom level, there are the housing authority's two million public tenants; the new middle class lives in flats bought at subsidised prices from government; and the official class and the expatriates also live in subsidised accommodation. The housing market has broken down simply because Hong Kong is the most crowded place on earth, with a population density twenty times that of Britain, in parts as high as one-third of a million people per square mile. The Wah Fu estate, on the southern tip of Hong Kong island, houses 52,000 people, roughly the population of Maidenhead but in a fraction of the space. Three-quarters of the land area of Hong Kong is mountainous, marshy or otherwise unsuitable for habitation. As Sir Murray MacLehose stated in his report to the Legislative Council in 1981: 'We are a tiny territory whose terrain seems specially designed to impede development on land.'

Had Hong Kong's population grown at a natural rate from 1945 onwards, the problem could probably have been solved. The Hong Kong to which many of its pre-war population returned in 1945 was well equipped in one sense. For the first and probably the last time in its existence, there was enough housing—something like 750,000 dwellings for 600,000 people. Unfortunately, much of the property had been damaged or had deteriorated during the war and needed repair. The pace of post-war reconstruction was slow and did not take into account the phenomenon that has dogged the government's housing programme ever since—refugees. In the five years after the war the population of Hong Kong ballooned four times to 2.4 million. The communist takeover of China in 1949 and the ensuing chaos persuaded many mainland Chinese to chance their luck in Hong Kong. They settled wherever they could, on any flat piece of land, and put up makeshift shacks. Squatting became a normal way of life for hundreds of thousands of people. The government did nothing on the grounds that it did not have to do anything: after all, these people had not been invited so why should the Hong Kong taxpayer do anything for them. Market forces, it was felt, would somehow or other sort out the mess. As the squatter settlements multiplied, taking over more and more land, disease and public health became a problem. Furthermore, squatters often took over land earmarked for development. The government's initial reaction was to evict them from any site they settled on, but since they merely set up house elsewhere, it was hardly a solution. Events forced the government into action.

On Christmas Eve, 1953 a fire swept through a squatter encampment at Shep Kip Mei in Kowloon, leaving 50,000 homeless. Having delayed for so long, the government now acted with resolution and efficiency. Within fifty-three days the Public Works Department had built a series of two-storey blocks to provide emergency housing for 35,000 of the fire victims. During the next year the government set up a Resettlement Department to

Twice the Area of the Grave

A true measure of the failure of the government's ambitious housing programme is the number of resettlement blocks still standing in Hong Kong. Run up in haste during the 1950s to provide temporary accommodation for people from squatter areas, 25,000 people still live in these blocks. The intention was that all of them should have been demolished by now: they were described in 1972 by the governor as 'unfit for human living'. The Lei Cheng Uk estate is one such block. Put up in 1954, its facilities are grotesquely inadequate. None of the flats has a toilet, few have kitchens. Water supplies are communal and often break down. An average family of five to six people live in 120sq ft of space; their rent is about £10 a month.

Elsie Elliott, who has campaigned for these blocks to be torn down, describes them thus:

> If you're living in a room that is, say, 80sq ft with five other people, you'd be living in worse conditions than the minimum for prisoners in America. They went on strike and even took the prison authorities to court. And they had something like twice the space some of our people are living in. Our people aren't prisoners.

Effectively, some of them are. Mrs Chan has been living at Lei Cheng Uk for twenty years. She has no family and no income—only a little money saved from the days when she had a job. She pays £1 a month in rent and in return gets a space about the size of a broom cupboard to live in. As one social worker put it, 'it's twice the area of a grave'. There is little hope for Mrs Chan and others like her. Lei Cheng Uk was supposed to have been pulled down—but recently the government announced that it won't be rebuilt for fifteen years. Mrs Chan has a long wait ahead of her.

rehouse squatters. The blocks built by the department, the so-called 'biscuit boxes' were erected at great speed. It is a measure of the scale of Hong Kong's housing problem that these blocks, intended for temporary occupation, are still there, a familiar sight on the Hong Kong skyline. A housing authority was also set up to provide a better class of accommodation for the residents of seedy private tenement blocks. Thus began one of the most ambitious housing programmes in the world—one that was to lead the government down the long road to involvement in social welfare. By 1982 the Housing Authority controlled nearly half a million flats. Undoubtedly it has been an impressive building programme, yet throughout its thirty-year history it has been plagued by setbacks. Each time the housing problem has seemed to be within grasp of solution, fresh immigration has snatched away the fruits of victory. As a result, the colony's immigration policy, increasingly restrictive over the years, has become an important weapon in the government's armoury of welfare policies.

Initially, the 'barren island' had need of people to build it up and make it work, and, in addition, China had insisted in the treaty which leased Hong Kong to Britain that its people should have the right to come and go as they pleased. Since then, many have come, but few have gone. Effectively that clause of the treaty has been abandoned by mutual consent. After the first wave of immigration in the 1940s, the open-door policy was marginally tightened up in the 1950s, but by then the communist government in China had stabilised and, with the return of order to the villages and cities of the south, the pace of immigration slackened of its own accord.

The 1960's Cultural Revolution sparked off a new wave of mass emigration. The Hong Kong government responded once again by tightening up the rules. It was by no means a tough policy, but it remained in force until 1980. Nicknamed 'touchbase', the policy would be hard to describe in anything but sporting terms, as a complicated game. Under it, anyone caught on the border was handed back to the Chinese authorities. If, however, an immigrant managed to get into the urban area, and made contact with friends or relations (i.e. touch a base), he or she was allowed to stay. It was a curious way of running an immigration policy, but it seemed to work. Once again, when the disorder of the Cultural Revolution ended, the pressure to get out eased.

By 1980 the pressure had built up again, as greater freedom of movement within China and increasing contacts with the rest of the world made China's people more aware of the better living standards enjoyed in Hong Kong. The touchbase policy made for reasonable odds, as the figures show. In 1977 1,800 out of an estimated 8,400 illegals were caught crossing the border and sent back; in 1978 28,100 got in while 8,200 were caught; and in 1979 107,700 made the crossing successfully while another 90,000 were arrested at the border. By the middle of 1980 about 3,500 illegal immigrants were arriving in Hong Kong every day. The overstretched police and army units simply couldn't hold the line.

It was clear that the colony would collapse if the flow continued at that rate. The Chinese authorities were getting worried too: some of the communes near the border had lost two-thirds of their workforce. By

mutual—but unspoken—agreement between the two governments, the touchbase policy was replaced by much tougher measures. From 23 October 1980 all illegal immigrants from China were returned, regardless of where they were caught; and the whole population of Hong Kong was given three days in which to register for identity cards. Not having an identity card was virtually a passport back to China, since no one could get a job or a house from that day on without producing ID. The news travelled fast into China and the effect was sudden and dramatic. From a daily average of 450 arrests in September, the border police arrested an average of only twenty-five a day in November. The Chinese authorities have borne the brunt of policing the new policy. It is estimated by the British officers in charge of the border area that of any five illegal immigrants, three are stopped by the Chinese, one by the British, and one gets through.

Wah Fu Estate—a density over twenty times that of Britain.

Illegal immigrants are still coming in, though these days it is only the foolish who attempt a direct crossing of the border fence. The latest method of entry is by high-powered speedboat onto one of Hong Kong's many small islands, but this is an option available only to the wealthy since a run apparently costs around £2,000. The respite may be only temporary if China's measures to revitalise her economy fail. An important factor in the slowing down of immigration has been the building of a special economic zone in Shum Zhum, just across the border from Hong Kong. It offers the chance of a much better standard of living to the people of Gwuangdong province, and thereby lessens the urge to look for the better life in Hong

Kong. The building of the zone has had an interesting side effect on the job of the British border guards. The majority of illegal immigrants now come from the interior of China, provinces where the benefits of the special economic zones have not penetrated, but where rumours of Hong Kong's good life have. This has resulted in several of the interrogating police officers having to learn the dialects of the interior so that they can question the immigrants. The dialect may have changed but the motivation has not. One immigrant, asked why he was trying to get to Hong Kong, replied simply: 'Hong Kong is place where man eat fat pork'.

That simple motivation has forced Hong Kong to cater for infinitely more people than would have been thought possible a century ago. No one knows the exact figure, but the best estimate is about five and a half million. About 55,000 legal immigrants are still arriving each year, mostly relations of Hong Kong residents. The first weapon in the government's social policy—immigration control—has only belatedly been successful, but it is vital, for each new immigrant threatens the standard of living of the rest of the population. And whatever threatens living standards indirectly threatens government. Government officials reason that if the population could riot over a one penny rise in fares on the Star ferry, what would they do if they were forced to contemplate a future that included no possibility of better living conditions?

Sir Murray MacLehose's government made housing a central issue. Former civil servant John Walden remembers taking Sir Murray round a resettlement block early in his term of office: 'He saw for himself the conditions in which people were living. He was very concerned; he thought that bad housing was at the root of so many of our problems here. So he gave the whole thing a great boot forward.' The ten-year housing programme was launched by Sir Murray with the aim of breaking the back of Hong Kong's housing problem. It was an attack from several angles. The problem of mass immigration was tackled by tightening up the immigration laws and allocating greater resources to catching illegals. The Marine Police currently deploys twenty high-speed launches a day in the search for illegal immigrants, and Royal Navy hovercraft and patrol boats back them up. The second arm of MacLehose's policy was to try to keep squatting under control.

In one sense squatting has now become an accepted part of the official housing policy. Certain squats have been legalised: if the huts have numbers painted on them, they are allowed to remain. It is an acceptance of the fact that squatter huts are going to remain a part, albeit near the bottom, of Hong Kong's housing stock for many years to come. Illegal squatters are less fortunate. The government employs squatter control units, gangs of workmen equipped with bulldozers and crowbars whose job it is to pull down illegally built huts, or illegal extensions to existing legal huts. They go about their work with a certain cool detachment, but it is a harrowing sight to watch them in action. They descend on illegal huts, which are normally made of a few supporting timbers and corrugated iron, politely move the inhabitants and their possessions out, then systematically knock the place to pieces. It is done with little emotion on either side: the control unit seems neither to take much pleasure in its work, nor to be worried by it. The squatters regard it as the luck of the draw even though they may have spent £2,000 on a hut. Something like 250 huts a week are knocked down by the control units—but even that tally is not enough to stop new ones springing up.

It all seems part of a curious ritual. Many of the huts are built by the criminal mafias of Hong Kong, the Triads. For £2,000 you get a hut, primitive sanitation, a risky power line and water. What government cannot provide the Triads will. Urban Councillor Elsie Elliott, who is no fan of the government's housing policy, described the Triads as 'a sort of government within a government. They have their own housing office, they have their own private supplies of electricity and water. They're in it for the money, and they make a lot of it.' She implies that Triad activity is tolerated because it is fulfilling a need that government cannot meet.

Having your house demolished while you watch is by no means the worst hazard that can befall a squatter. The disaster that launched Hong Kong on its original housing programme, fire, is still a regular occurrence. The officials in charge of clearing up the debris after a fire talk of a fire 'season' as we would of a football or a baseball season. The huts are crowded together without fire breaks, and erratic electricity supplies and the use of kerosene cooking stoves mean that fires break out easily. During the hot season they occur several times a week. The authorities keep a meticulously accurate log of fire casualties: in the eighteen months from October 1979 2,152 were made homeless by a fire at Lei Yue Mun; 4,366 at Ma Chai Hang; 1,076 at Chai Wan; 2,780 at Ping Yeung; and 6,374 at Tai Hom Wor. In that same period a total of more than 21,000 were made homeless as a result of fire. The housing authority is fighting an uphill battle: for every two homes they build, one more person is made homeless by fire.

Some fires are started deliberately in an attempt to force the government to rehouse the victims. After a fire the procedure is always the same: the squatters register with a government agency, and have to prove that they are real fire victims. ID is checked carefully as some people try to jump the housing queue by pretending to be fire victims. Once the authorities are satisfied the case is genuine, some help is given. It comes in the form of a rolled-up mat, a couple of blankets and some cooking utensils. With that the squatter is expected to start life again.

The next level up in housing, to which many of those without a place in the housing queue will be sent, is a Temporary Housing Area. It is spelt with capital letters because it is one of the temporary solutions to housing problems that seems to have become permanent. The THAs are virtually refugee camps, with fairly primitive facilities. There are more than forty of them dotted around Hong Kong, housing about 90,000 people. Such is the demand that space for a further 50,000 people is planned. It is very much 'do-it-yourself' housing: the government provides a basic wooden structure, about the size of two garden sheds one on top of the other. The squatters are given a supply of wood, corrugated iron and tools and told to get on with it. Proper water supplies, sanitation and power are supplied to each dwelling, but it is a hard life. A family of three are expected to live in about 75sq ft and pay about £6 a month for the privilege. It's a long way off

Sha Tin—the promise of a better tomorrow.

decent housing, but it's better than the disease-ridden squalor of a squatter village.

Hong Kong's housing policy shouldn't be seen entirely in negative terms. The government has realised the need for good-quality, low-price, permanent accommodation, but the only part of Hong Kong which can be built on is the New Territories; by 1997, over half the population will be living there. The government has undertaken a massive construction programme, mainly on reclaimed land, and it is estimated that one million people are now living on land clawed back from the sea. Sha Tin is one of three new cities that are springing up in the New Territories. Once a peaceful inlet of fishing villages, it is the showpiece of the new development scheme, with an intended population of over three-quarters of a million people by 1990. Building began in 1973 and, to give an idea of the scale of the project, one family is moving into Sha Tin every twelve minutes over the seventeen years of the project. Thirty villages are being swallowed up by the city as it expands.

It is social engineering on a massive scale, however much officials in charge dislike the phrase. Early on mistakes were made in planning and now the aim is to produce a balanced community. Fifty-seven per cent of the housing will be public, forty-three per cent private, and the government has encouraged private developers so as to provide a better social mix. The aim is to get everyone from paupers to millionaires living in Sha Tin. Typical conditions would horrify a Westerner accustomed to more space, but by

85

The Master Builder

The government Land Rover lurched from side to side as we bumped across an uneven track to the plateau above Sha Tin new town. Patrick Hase changed gear, pushed his glasses back up his nose and waved an expansive arm across 'his' town: 'Here on this hill, this is a large home ownership estate. These are estates the government is building and then selling at cost price to people within a stated income range.' We are being given the conducted tour of Sha Tin from the man in charge of this extraordinary creation. Hase has his lecture off pat, and always takes visitors up to a small observation point above the town to illustrate his points. Like a retired general re-fighting old battles over the dinner table, he waves his arms to take in the valley from one end to the other, pointing out places of interest. He is District Officer for Sha Tin but not exactly what one would expect of such a colonial title. His academic qualifications include a PhD in medieval history. He admits that it is a bit odd:

> That I am here is basically a historical accident of course. I took a job as an administrative officer with the Hong Kong government because it was an interesting one, full of scope. It is a job you can give all your strength and all your time to. I think I can serve the people by building them the best town possible, making sure that it is as close to the needs of the people as I can conceivably get it.

He possesses a quality of boundless self-confidence, combined with the conviction that he is right, and that he is doing a good job. Patrick Hase knows that he is the last frontiersman of a contracting empire, but it doesn't seem to affect his attitude—he has a job to do and he's going to get on with it as best as he can. One regular group of visitors to Sha Tin are the Chinese administrators who are doing a similar job in China. 'They want to come and see how to get it right before they do it,' he says.

Hong Kong standards Sha Tin has a great deal to offer. The Wo Che estate, a public high-density housing area, provides homes for 40,000 people. An average flat is about 600sq ft, about half the living area of an English semi-detached house: in it live as many as nine people. It is terribly crowded, but it's a great advance on a squatter hut or a refugee camp.

Most of Hong Kong's population will probably never own their own homes: at Sha Tin the government is trying to meet the aspiration for home ownership. Flats are sold off at subsidised rates well below their market value. Prices are pegged to recovering the actual construction costs and an element of the value of the land involved. A condition of the sale is that the flat may not be sold again for five years. For what's on offer, the prices aren't cheap. A 700sq ft flat sells for about £30,000. Eligibility to buy is restricted to people who have been in Hong Kong for some time, but the scheme is so popular that the government has to allocate the flats by ballot. The obvious policy aim is to create a new middle class with a real stake in the future of Hong Kong.

Aside from encouraging private developers to come in and build, the government's aim is to make Sha Tin a self-sufficient working town, with its own schools, shops, restaurants, public transport and car parks. The government has had less success in persuading business to set up shop in Sha Tin to provide a local employment base. At present four out of five of Sha Tin's working population commutes to Kowloon or Hong Kong Island, but the government hopes that will change as employers move in to the city.

It sounds like a Western urban planner's nightmare, but the problems of alienation and vandalism that such a scheme might encounter elsewhere don't seem to apply to Hong Kong. District Officer Patrick Hase says,

> We're lucky in that we are dealing with a Chinese population who tend to knit together very quickly. Vandalism is just not part of the Chinese culture. The Chinese feel there's very little point in it. If they are going to write on walls, it will be done with the best handwriting they can do. You will sometimes find people who practise their calligraphy on a spare wall. But 'Kilroy was here'—no, that's not in the culture.

Sha Tin is budgeted at well over £1 billion for the government share alone. Over the whole colony, the housing programme envisages construction of 180,000 flats for rent and sale over the next five years. But the government is in the position of the Red Queen in *Alice in Wonderland*, running as fast as it can to stay in the same place. Critics claim that the government has failed in what has been seen for the last ten years as the central problem confronting it. Urban Councillor Elsie Elliott, a persistent critic of government welfare policies, suggests:

> We are in a worse position now than at the start of the housing programme in the early seventies. There are about a million people living in squatter huts, and I would say another two million living in inferior public housing, or living in private housing in the most appalling conditions.

Not everyone would agree with her exact figures: few would dispute that
something like half the population of Hong Kong is living in inadequate
housing.

Though the government is justifiably proud of its achievements, it too
has to acknowledge that the ten-year programme has failed. John Walden, a
former civil servant, was in on the beginning of that.

The ten-year housing programme was due to end in 1982. The
target—and a lot of publicity was given to it at the beginning—was 1.8
million people housed in ten years. I think we'll be lucky to reach half
that number.

Walden attributes the cause to a failure of will on the part of government:

There just wasn't that collective determination to achieve the results.
Some civil servants thought the governor was being too ambitious and
that if government pushed housing so hard it might take the bottom
out of real-estate development in the private sector.

When Sir Murray MacLehose launched the programme, he said of the
colony's housing problem: 'It offends alike our humanity, our civic pride,
our political good sense.' Now a decade on and several billion pounds later,
housing is still a problem. As an additional measure because demand for

housing still outstrips supply, the government has had to impose rent controls. It has found that once you start intervening it is very difficult to stop. More money spent on housing means more inflation or more taxes—neither of which would be politically acceptable—but failing to break the back of the housing problem could sink the government. One businessman, an admirer of government policies, described the position with unconscious irony: 'The government's hand is everywhere, but it has a very light touch and often cannot be felt at all.'

If the new governor, Sir Edward Youde, cannot find a way of making the 'light touch' of government felt in the housing and welfare field, the credibility of the Hong Kong government could be called into question. Elsie Elliott sums up the effort made by government thus: 'One of the members of parliament who came here on a visit got it exactly right when he said, you have a housing programme but no policy. That's exactly it—we haven't got a policy.'

CHAPTER EIGHT

FROM THE WRONG END OF THE TELESCOPE

> Hong Kong is not a complete society, it has two contrasting sides. There are those who find Hong Kong an exciting, prosperous place to live in. They live up on the Peak, or up the hill somewhere; they're the rich people. And on the other side you'll find the poor, the people who just don't know where they're going. They live from hand to mouth and day to day; there's no future for them, no security.

As Urban Councillor Elsie Elliott points out, life is hard at the wrong end of the Hong Kong spectrum. There are no safety nets if you fall; the ruthless work ethic and the laissez-faire economic philosophy are seen as vital to the successful functioning of the system. If they failed there would be little else to sustain the dynamic progress of Hong Kong. The pressures of high-speed economic growth have produced a community in which traditional ethics are weakened, traditional loyalties strained. A high crime rate, and deep-seated corruption have all been part of the price Hong Kong has paid for its rapid transition to a major modern industrial state.

One would expect those at the bottom of the pile to organise themselves collectively in an effort to improve their lot. In nineteenth-century Europe, as a traditional society broke down under the pressure of the Industrial Revolution, workers retaliated by seeking new forms of organisation to protect their positions. The modern trades unions of the West grew out of the conscious need to redress, in a collective fashion, a balance of power that favoured the employer. At one time it seemed as if Hong Kong would follow the European pattern. Craftsmen's guilds were formed in the 1920s, aimed at protecting the interests of skilled workers. There was a general strike in 1922, instigated by the Chinese Seamen's Union of Hong Kong, which involved 120,000 men and was eventually settled on terms favourable to the union.

Today the trades unions have withered and are an insignificant part of the social structure. In 1981 there were 366 trades unions registered in Hong Kong, with only 361,940 members between them, out of a total labour force of 2.5 million. Given the appalling conditions in many of Hong Kong's manufacturing industries and the growth of an educated and sophisticated workforce, the failure of the unions is surprising.

One factor has been the influence of events elsewhere: for the labour

Lam Tin market.

unions, as for everyone else in Hong Kong, events in other countries have had a disproportionate impact inside the colony. The rise to power of the Nationalists in China after the 1911 revolution brought the new industrial unions into politics. Sun Yat Sen, the founder of the Nationalist or Kuomintang Party, went out of his way to gain the political support of organised labour for the revolution. At the same time, the newly founded Communist Party of China set up a Labour Secretariat whose job it was to organise trades unions. Both nationalists and communists wooed the unions of Hong Kong for their support. The unions in turn became more interested in political issues than industrial matters. A government report in 1939 noted that the unions 'took on a more and more leftish complexion and became frankly revolutionary, nationalistic and anti-foreign'.

The split between the Nationalists and the Communists in 1927 meant inevitably that the unions in Hong Kong, which were mostly controlled from outside by one or other party, were drawn into the developing battle for the control of China. The Hong Kong government responded by passing the Illegal Strikes and Lockout Ordinance. This outlawed sympathy strikes or secondary action of any sort, and made illegal the foreign control of any Hong Kong union. Although the act was never invoked it did much to put the unions on the defensive.

The world trade depression of the 1930s was a more serious blow to the unions: throughout the decade there was a surplus of labour and few of the unions had enough industrial experience or strength to be able to counteract the negotiating power of the employers. The upheaval of the Japanese invasion, followed by renewed civil war in China, in which communist and nationalist unions found their sympathies divided according to political loyalties, effectively rendered the unions powerless in the years immediately after the war. The influx of refugees from China meant that labour was plentiful and hungry—hardly ideal conditions for union recruiting—and the setting up of a series of competing unions in the same industry—one communist, one Kuomintang or nationalist—did little to endear trades unions to Hong Kong's workforce. Unions were needed to counter the appalling working conditions which prevailed as Hong Kong struggled to rebuild its industrial base, but when joining a union meant declaring for one side or the other in the Chinese civil war, many workers felt they were better off out of the battle; that, after all, was one of the reasons they had fled to Hong Kong.

The British government made half-hearted attempts to encourage 'responsible' trades unionism along British lines, in the hope of introducing collective bargaining into the chaos. Neither employers nor unions were keen on this. It suited the employers to have a fragmented workforce; and the unions were keener on fighting each other for membership on political grounds than uniting to fight employers. In 1949 two federations of labour were set up—the Hong Kong Federation of Trades Unions, which was communist run, and the Nationalist managed Hong Kong and Kowloon Trades Council. In essence, that split has remained to the present day.

A pre-war description of Hong Kong's trades unions in a government report in 1939 could as well describe their condition in the decades after the war: 'Little more than friendly societies concerned more with the provision of funeral expenses for the dead than the improvement of the conditions of the living.' The pro-Peking group of unions have become communist unions in the sense recognised in China: they provide welfare, educational and recreational services for their members but involve themselves little in real industrial disputes. They have gone even further and now see their role in overtly political terms. Although they organised demonstrations on the streets of Hong Kong during the 1960's Cultural Revolution, they now see it as their duty to keep the peace so that trade between Hong Kong and China is not disrupted. It is a truly communist view of the union role, but of little help to its members in terms of wages and conditions. The pro-Nationalist federation limits its activities to legal advice, education for workers and agitating on behalf of Nationalist Taiwan. Workers' relationships with employers, it would seem, can be left to look after themselves.

The only part of Hong Kong's labour force where unions have flourished is the public sector. White-collar unionism has strengthened its hold among groups like teachers and local government workers, as in many other countries of the world. Overall union membership in Hong Kong has declined, however, from 25 per cent to 23 per cent of the workforce in four years. A new organisation has sprung up which may reverse the pattern— the oddly named Christian Industrial Committee. More a pressure group than a trades union, the CIC liaises between traditional unions and gives

The Squeeze

In the pidgin English of the China coast in the eighteenth century, 'squeegee' meant being put in prison, and not being let out until you paid your captor some money. In time it seems this word may have been incorporated into the English language. The Oxford Dictionary is not clear where the word 'squeeze' comes from, but this seems a likely explanation. The Western merchants on the China coast applied the phrase to the sums they had to pay to their Chinese business partners before any transactions to facilitate trade could be carried out. Taking a percentage of the gross from the opium trade was massively profitable. Wu Ping Chan, who was Jardine's Chinese partner, was estimated to be worth £4.5 million in 1834.

The tradition of the squeeze has remained in Hong Kong to this day. The Triad which 'owns' a given street will extract a percentage from any legitimate trader on that street—including the hawkers and shoe-shine boys. Most people pay up rather than face Triad enforcers. The more sophisticated Triads run rackets at a higher level. Loan sharking is a favourite one; running illegal gambling another. At this level, the operations begin to merge, as in the case of organised crime in America, into legitimate business. Take the case of the green public minibuses which are the unique Hong Kong compromise between buses and taxis. They are franchised by government and run where they like, charge what the market will bear and stop whenever the passengers ask. The Triads have moved in on the most profitable runs and started their own franchise system, whereby they determine who takes which run and extract a percentage of the profits.

The geographical organisation of the Triads—they control a particular street or block—presents its own problems. According to one story, the Triads are having difficulty in deciding who should hold the 'franchise' for organising petty theft on the Mass Transit Railway—it runs through too many Triad boundaries. Thus, in theory, the MTR is one of the safest means of transport in the world: until, that is, the Triads organise themselves.

them the research and information with which to negotiate. Its director, Lau Chin Shek, sees it as filling a gap:

> The unions aren't doing the job of representing workers' interests through collective bargaining. If the trades unions want to be more effective, they should cater to the needs of the local people, hear the voice of the grass roots and fight for real benefits in concrete terms rather than involve themselves in politics.

Instead of taking on the whole range of trades union activities, the CIC has decided to concentrate on specific issues. Its first target was industrial safety.

The construction industry is big business in Hong Kong, and with so much pressure on workers to get a job done quickly, a high accident rate is inevitable. On many sites workers do not wear proper safety clothing like hard hats. For the construction companies the benefits of working fast are enormous: finishing a contract early earns a big bonus. The fine for failing to meet industrial safety standards is low—an accident may cost the company as little as £100 in fines. Mr Lau says, 'We want the fine to be high enough to be a real deterrent. Maybe not only a fine, but imprisonment too for the construction manager if he doesn't keep to safety regulations.' The CIC is also pressing the government to take a more active part in policing safety standards: only 140 inspectors are employed to keep an eye on safety. The CIC has won some small victories: in October 1980 the fines for violations of safety legislation were increased five-fold and an Industrial Safety Committee with representatives from industry and government was set up. Not unnaturally the CIC claims the credit.

To be fair to government, it has urged employers to provide better and safer working conditions over the years. It has promoted 'responsible' trades unionism in the public sector and risked the wrath of the Chinese business community by legislating for better holidays. It sees its role in labour relations as conciliation—'to anticipate and avoid conflict, to prevent grievances building up into major disputes . . . and to reduce obvious sources of friction by gradual legislative amendment'.

But government can do little faced with a disorganised situation where there are two taxi drivers' unions, one for Hong Kong, one for Kowloon; where there are catering unions based on the place of origin of the member; where numerous small unions exist, such as the Hong Kong Edible Bird's Nest Workers Union with twenty-one members, or the Hong Kong and Kowloon Camphor Wood Trunk Workers Union with fourteen members. The splintered nature of organised labour in Hong Kong means that someone has to watch over the workers' interests.

Apart from this historical legacy of political division, another factor weakens the unions. The economy of Hong Kong is dominated by small businesses. Only a handful of companies employ more than 200 workers, and there are very few large employers in the private sector. The small companies are run on a firmly paternalistic basis. The business is seen as an extension of the family: thus, in return for the loyalty of the worker, the

Night-time in the Wanchai.

master provides housing, food and other benefits. Although that would be unacceptable to workers in the Western world, it is considered quite normal by the Chinese. As the chairman of one large Chinese industrial concern said recently: 'Paternalism is part and parcel of the cultures of Asia and I see no reason for it being dropped.' Traditional Confucian thinking emphasises vertical loyalty from son to father or employee to boss rather than the horizontal loyalty to fellow workers. The Chinese worker does not regard himself as in a 'them' and 'us' position. He does not want a larger share of someone else's cake but rather aspires to a cake of his own. Why, he would reason, be a wage slave when you can be an owner of capital?

If the Chinese working class have shown themselves seemingly incapable of collective action on the industrial front, the story is rather different in another area. The organisation of groups of people for criminal purposes is a major element of modern Hong Kong—and one which the colony's police force seems incapable of countering. Crime in Hong Kong is largely run by the Triads, a Chinese version of the Mafia, imported into Hong Kong from mainland China and now exported again to Chinese communities all over the world. The official line in Hong Kong is that the Triads are not a massive criminal organisation in the Mafia sense, but rather, as one policeman put it, 'a self-help society, an association rather than an organisation'. No one would dispute that the Triads are behind most of the organised crime in Hong Kong. The police say that about 60 per cent of those sent to prison in Hong Kong claim Triad affiliations.

The Triads have a long history, although the modern-day criminal organisations—or associations—are far removed in their purpose from the founders of the Triad movement. Founded in the seventeenth century after the overthrow of the Ming dynasty, the first Triad was dedicated to its restoration and had as its slogan 'Fan Ching fu Ming'—'Overthrow the Ching and restore the Ming'. For years Triads retained their political motivation, adding to it the Robin Hood spirit by taking from the rich and giving to the poor. However, by the nineteenth century the Triads had degenerated into secret societies of bandits looking after their own interests in the increasingly chaotic conditions of China. They remained secret societies with complicated rituals for inauguration run by a hierarchic leadership.

When the British took over Hong Kong and announced an open-door immigration policy, several of the Triads of south China used the opportunity to escape from the persecution of the authorities on the mainland. The first anti-Triad legislation was enacted by the British only three years after the setting up of Hong Kong. It seems to have had little effect. In the late nineteenth century Triads still retained peripheral respectability. Although much of their behaviour was pure banditry, they also expressed many of the revolutionary and nationalistic feelings of the Chinese. Sun Yat Sen, the founder of the Nationalist Party, was a Triad. His successor, Chiang Kai Shek, made use of Triads as an arm of the state's intelligence service. A Triad formed by one of his generals, the 14K, moved its operations to Hong Kong after the communist takeover, and has now become one of the major criminal influences in the colony.

No one knows how many Triad members there are in Hong Kong, or how significant such a number would be. In 1960 Police Commissioner Henry Heath estimated that there were 500,000 Triad members in Hong Kong. Most members are probably inactive, but even they are thought to be capable of supporting their leaders in an emergency. Big Triads like 14K have an estimated 20,000 members and a large-scale organisation; the tiny Ching Wah Se Triad has only thirty members and is believed to operate in an area bounded by two streets.

Superintendent Ben Munford, the head of Hong Kong's Police Anti-Triad Division, regards the Triads as a means of carving up criminal patches so that everyone gets a slice. Each Triad has its own territory, and woe betide anyone who comes into that area to commit a crime: 'They're going to come and tap you on the shoulder and there will be the traditional Triad question, where do you belong brother?' The interloper has a choice: he can either leave the area or join the local Triad, or he can make a deal whereby a proportion of his 'earnings' goes to the resident Triad. It's all very formal and tidy. Businesses like illegal gambling, bars, bowling alleys, amusement arcades—all these will attract the attention of the local Triad as potential sources of revenue.

The Hong Kong police have repeatedly claimed to be in control of the Triads. One Hong Kong policeman, writing after the 1956 riots—during which the Triads had been responsible for stirring up trouble—claimed that 'shortly afterwards, the back of the Triad movement was broken by arrests,

The Fakers

Hong Kong is famous as a shoppers' paradise—the place where you can buy a product cheaper than anywhere else in the world. On every street corner there are small booths selling watches, cameras, perfume, jeans, handbags and a thousand other gifts to take home. Many of them aren't quite what they seem for one of Hong Kong's most flourishing industries is the manufacture of fakes: Gucci bags that never saw Rome, Sony tapes that aren't Sony tapes, Levi jeans that come from the back streets of Kowloon. Many a visitor has picked up a bargain in Hong Kong only to find out on getting home that it doesn't work or falls to pieces. Hong Kong's Principal Trade Investigator, John Howard, isn't sympathetic: 'What do you expect for half price—the real thing?' His office has a marvellous black museum of fake goods which they have seized in raids on factories and stores. The standard of fakery is extremely high. John Howard holds the genuine article in one hand, the fake in the other; then switches them round and defies you to guess which is which.

The most extraordinary products are faked: the Trade Investigation Department has bust a racket making fake Lucozade, which can't have been very profitable. The high quality of some fakes may be explained by the fact that, in some cases, both phoney and real come from the same factory. Howard explains: 'In many cases we get normally legitimate manufacturers who will take a chance on an illegitimate order in the hope of getting it shipped before information is given to this department.' Both the real thing and the fake are made in the same building—but leave by different exits. Faking is big business: the Trade Investigation Department gets on average one complaint a day, and investigated 300 complaints in the first nine months of 1981. In the course of their inquiries they seized fake goods worth almost £2 million. The penalties have been stepped up in response to the amount of counterfeiting that goes on: but despite a five-fold increase in fines, the fakers keep going. It is a drop in the ocean of Hong Kong's legitimate trade—indeed nowadays some of the complaints come from Hong Kong based companies—but it is a part of free enterprise that the government thinks is too free. One faker was so convinced of the quality of his Gucci bags that he sold them in Hong Kong at a higher price than the real thing.

The Mass Transit Railway—Hong Kong's underground.

imprisonment and deportation. Within two or three years their organisation was shattered.' Like many police statements about the Triads, it was over-optimistic. In the next five years 10,500 Triad members were arrested—with no noticeable effect on Triad activities. In July 1973 a further attempt to 'break the Triads for once and for all' was made. Impressive numbers of people were arrested, but today the Triads are as strong as ever.

They have become a worse problem since the advent of a flourishing world-wide drug market. The enormous profits to be made from heroin manufacture and transportation have reversed any possible decline in the Triads' fortunes. Hong Kong is an important entrepôt in the flow of heroin from the Golden Triangle of South East Asia to American and Europe. One customs officer estimated that, in terms of value, heroin was the most important product to pass through Hong Kong's Kai Tak airport. The trade is controlled by Triads, and has resulted in an extension of their influence into quite new areas. Superintendent Munford is realistic enough to admit that they are a powerful force and will continue to be for a long time. Fighting them is not easy:

> It is like trying to pick up lumps of mercury. You might be able to see it there; you go to pick it up and you get a lot of it, but in doing so you will spread a lot around. And lots of little pieces are very difficult to pick up. The moment you turn your back it all runs together again.

Critics of the police, like Elsie Elliott, claim the Triads could be beaten if a determined effort was made. She points to the case of mainland China where ruthless Communist Party action against Triads in 1949 wiped them out completely.

> One policeman told me quite frankly that they could stamp out the drug trade and Triads any time they wanted to. And I said, 'Well why don't you?' He said, 'nobody would allow us to do that, the drug trade is controlled at such a high level that any policeman who tried to do anything would be in the soup.'

This extravagant-sounding claim has been born out by recent events. Turning a blind eye to the drug trade, and even facilitating its business, has made many Hong Kong policemen rich over the years. Systematic and organised corruption, extending high up in the ranks of the police force, has been one of the reasons why the Triads have not been broken.

The exposure of corruption in Hong Kong's police force is one of the few things the world knows about Hong Kong. The sensational flight of Chief Superintendent Peter Godber in 1973, after he had been asked to explain the large sums of money in his bank accounts tore the lid off corruption. Godber had £300,000 in various accounts and was unable to explain it away. Eventually he was brought back to Hong Kong and sentenced to four years in jail for corruptly accepting HK$25,000 (about £2,500). It was widely believed at the time that Godber had stashed away some £4 million in bribes. Several more detectives went to prison—or fled—in the purge that followed. Although Godber and the British officers charged were the ones who got all the headlines, some of the junior Chinese officers are alleged to have made even more out of the drugs trade. One Chinese police sergeant with an impeccable record (he had been awarded the Colonial Police Medal) who had recently retired from the force, fled from Hong Kong to Canada in November 1974 before the anti-corruption squad could arrest him. The magazine Newsweek claimed that he had been the Mr Big of the drugs business and had personally amassed a fortune of $600,000,000. Many other underpaid Chinese police officers found the bribes from the drug racketeers a useful way of supplementing their incomes.

The shock to the colony's system was enormous. The first reaction was to claim that only a minority of policemen were involved and that the matter should be a subject for internal discipline. That position soon became untenable under the pressure of public criticism, and the government decided to set up the Independent Commission Against Corruption— the ICAC. Its duty was to root out corruption, not just in the police force but in other areas as well. It began well with a heavy attack on the web of crooked policemen, but its activities made it unpopular with the police and rather too popular with the public. Huge numbers of complaints were made by the public, who had no particular affection for a police force which was widely believed to be arrogant and to have set itself above the law it was supposed to be defending. The police reacted vigorously to the ICAC's inquiries.

Hong Kong police patrol boat.

In November 1977 thousands of policemen staged a demonstration outside police headquarters and several dozen officers broke into the ICAC office in Hutchison House. They demanded that the commission lay off the police force. In an action for which he was more widely criticised than at any time during his governorship, Sir Murray agreed to a partial amnesty on corruption. It was seen as the reaction of a frightened government, giving in to blackmail. At least eighty-three anti-corruption cases, involving some 200 individuals, were covered by the amnesty. The governor rather lamely explained his action by saying that, 'in the force as a whole attitudes have been affected by some genuine grievances and by a sense of ill-usage as well as by misunderstandings'.

In January 1978, in an attempt to restore government and police credibility, Sir Murray invited a team of three senior British police officers to come to Hong Kong and advise him on any necessary reforms. The effect of this announcement was somewhat diminished by the team's leader, Mr Crane, the Inspector of Constabulary, who declared on arrival that, 'Our job is not to inquire into the affairs of the Hong Kong police,' but 'to assist the force in finding ways and means to meet their current problems.' It wasn't an attitude calculated to inspire confidence; to the sceptical public, it looked like a cover up.

Before the setting up of the ICAC, the prevention of corruption had been a job for the Hong Kong Police Force. As the government's official handout on the ICAC rather delicately words it, 'it became clear that this

The rotten apple—anti-corruption poster.

ordinance . . . was not effective in the particular circumstances of Hong Kong'. Since the vast majority of corruption cases involved the police, it was clear that an outside body was needed to handle complaints. The ICAC, set up in February 1974, was not a part of the police force but an independent organisation reporting directly to the governor. However, a limitation was imposed on its work which critics say has hampered it: prosecutions can only be undertaken with the approval of the attorney general, thereby removing much of the 'Independent' from the commission's title.

The ICAC now has a staff of 1,000, split into three departments. The operations department investigates complaints of corrupt behaviour; the prevention department gives advice to government departments and public bodies to help reduce the possibilities for corruption; and the community relations department exists to sell the idea of the commission to a sceptical public. This department runs the energetic advertising campaigns under the slogan 'Corruption Rots', aimed at showing the damage corruption can do to Hong Kong.

In its first five years the ICAC received 13,400 complaints and carried out 6,484 investigations; 1,322 arrests were made resulting in 861 convictions. The pace has since slackened: in 1981 the ICAC pursued a total of 95 cases, half of which resulted in convictions. The man in charge of the ICAC, Commissioner Peter Williams, explains that large-scale, syndicated corruption has now been wiped out—initially the ICAC's cases involved whole police stations engaged in organised corruption, whereas now the cases

Above: fishing junk in New Territories; below: the divided village of Sha Tau Kok — the border is the jetty; overleaf: a sailing junk.

involve individuals acting on their own. Peter Williams describes his job in these terms:

> My function as head of this organisation is really to be like a soldier, an old soldier—I must have blood on my sword, to put it in rather crude terms. That is, for the corrupt to create a sense of fear; for those who are thinking about being corrupt, a sense of apprehension; and for the vast majority of Hong Kongers, to be a symbol of the support our organisation can give the community.

He points to the increasing number of reports that come in from the public—2,000 in 1981—which he sees as a sign that the public has confidence in ICAC. Others see it as an indication that the problem has not yet been solved. Elsie Elliott is suspicious of the ICAC's claims of a dramatic improvement:

> Ostensibly there's been an effort to wipe out corruption. But the police and others complain quite rightly that the action is taken at the mid-level or lower level but not at the higher level. You pick out a person here and there and charge this one for taking a bribe of ten dollars and that one for taking a bribe of fifty dollars. It's useless.

Peter Williams acknowledges that he has not yet broken the back of corruption, but does point out that some big fish have been taken in anti-corruption drives. He is a pragmatist: 'We will never get rid of corruption. I think at the present time that this organisation, with the support of the administration and the people, has corruption at a level that is acceptable.'

The official view is, as Sir Murray put it, that Hong Kong has made 'enormous gains in public honesty since 1972'. But then the government is prepared to accept what is pragmatically possible. No civil servant in Britain would dare to say that there was an 'acceptable' level of corruption; in Hong Kong it's a realistic assessment of what government can and cannot do. The government recognises that its record on handling drug dealing, Triads and corruption isn't the best in the world: on the other hand, by the standards of South East Asia, it isn't a bad record. Hong Kong is certainly a markedly less evil society than many of its neighbours. The difference is that it is one in which traditional British virtues of decency and honest dealing are finding the going hard. When Mr Williams talks about acceptable levels, he means acceptable by Hong Kong not British standards, a point that was nicely illustrated in 1970. In that year the government put forward the Prevention of Bribery Bill under which it would be an offence to offer a public servant any entertainment. The Heung Yee Kuk, a New Territories assembly of village elders, protested strongly against the bill, and threatened to resign en masse if their custom of lavish entertainment of government officials became an offence. The government backed down. In Hong Kong you can only go so far in trying to prevent possible corruption.

CHAPTER NINE

THE CHANGING OF THE GUARD

The trouble is, people like you, you come to Hong Kong, you stay in Central, you live in an hotel, you meet Europeans and you think, my goodness, Hong Kong is run by the British. You know it's not really. We have a population of five and a bit million here; there's 26,000 UK residents, which is far less than the number of Chinese in New York. You wouldn't suggest New York was a Chinese run city would you?

Despite this comment from an old hand, Hong Kong does appear at first sight to be very British. Cars drive on the left, road signs are in English, traffic policemen wear British blue serge uniforms; many of the names are reassuringly English—Chater, Queen's Road, Repulse Bay. At twelve o'clock, as in Noël Coward's song, they sound the noonday gun from down by the Yacht Club. It is a touchingly British ritual, laid on for tourists by Jardine Matheson, the oldest of the British companies in Hong Kong. Three smart white-uniformed Chinese form the gun crew. The gun itself is a beautifully polished piece of light naval artillery. Nowadays they time the firing with the help of a quartz digital watch or the pips on the radio, but it doesn't detract from the traditional nature of the ceremony.

But the veneer is shallow; below the surface Hong Kong is a deeply Chinese city in its ways of working and thinking. 'Don't let anyone fool you,' says one journalist who has been here a long time, 'this town is Chinese and it's really run by the Chinese.' It is the Chinese who give Hong Kong its dynamism and pace. The old order of British colonial life and its rituals are crumbling.

The Hong Kong Club, where the Taipans or managers of the main British trading companies used to meet for a gin sling before lunch, has been pulled down to make way for new buildings. The Repulse Bay Hotel, where expatriate wives gathered for tea and bridge, has suffered the same fate. The Hong Kong Cricket Club used to have its ground in the middle of Hong Kong, under the shadow of the Bank of China building. In the 1960s a huge portrait of Chairman Mao, mounted on a hoarding on the side of the bank, stared down at the cricket ground. Today the hoarding has gone and so has the club—forced out because the land on which it stood was too valuable to be wasted on a mere game. It now perches on a slab of flattened land half-way up a hill, just outside the city centre in the Happy Valley. The new club has an air of impermanence, as if it expects to be moved on again.

Sooner or later someone will want to build offices or apartments on its flat space.

The members of the club are also impermanent. The demands of the modern multinational company are such that few expatriates spend more than a couple of years on any posting. The names of the club's teams seem to reflect the high membership turnover—one is called 'The Wanderers', another 'The Nomads'. A few of the club's members are long-term residents—the so-called 'belongers'. No one knows exactly what defines a belonger, but it is generally taken to mean that you have stayed in Hong Kong for more than seven years. Businessman Jeff Foster is by that standard a belonger: he has been a member of the club for thirteen years. Like many of the British belongers in the colony, he finds it difficult to define his relationship to the place: 'Obviously I regard myself as British, but also I consider Hong Kong to be my home, though always with the view that I will return to Britain to live eventually.' The word belonger clearly does not imply that you belong for ever. Karen Dewar, an expatriate in her twenties whose father is a senior executive with a trading company, Swire's, sums up the feelings of many:

> Hong Kong is my home, but my parents are British and therefore I am British, though I usually consider myself British Chinese because I live here. I am not sure now that I do consider Hong Kong to be my home any more. Truthfully I don't think any expatriate here knows where they belong. They are all very much the colonial; they live a colonial way of life and they are quite happy, but if you ask them where they belong, they just evade the question. I don't think anybody knows really.

The dilemma of the belongers is a modern one. Their ancestors had no problem defining themselves because they knew why they were there. The early British traders on the China coast had simple motives—a Shanghai based British merchant in a letter of 1840 explained it thus:

> In two or three years at furthest I hope to realise a fortune and get away . . . you must not expect men in my position to condemn themselves to prolonged exile in an unhealthy climate for the benefit of posterity. We are money-making practical men. Our business is to make money, as much and as fast as we can—and for this end all modes and means are good which the law allows.

In the early days it was relatively easy to make a fortune and take it back to Britain. James Matheson, one of the two founders of Jardine Matheson, spent thirty years out East establishing the company and making his fortune. In 1842 he relinquished control of Jardine's and retired to England. He became a member of parliament and in 1844 bought the Island of Lewes in Scotland as a country estate. The island, and his subsequent building works to improve it, cost him half a million pounds—at the time a massive amount of money.

Hong Kong Cricket Club.

Today the rewards aren't quite as attractive as that, but nor are the risks. For some the motivation is the same: there is no doubt that the rewards in Hong Kong are much better for almost any job than they are in the UK or America. One British merchant banker in his twenties, on a three-year posting from the head office of his bank in London, reckons that after paying tax and living expenses, he will save £100,000—money that will be used to buy a large house in London. To earn it, he was willing to work long hours for six days a week and pass up the sort of pleasures that London can offer and Hong Kong cannot: 'For £100,000 I can live without the Royal Shakespeare Company,' was the way he put it.

The lifestyle that goes with the large Hong Kong salaries is good, at least in material terms. In the old days the expatriate got a large house and an army of servants; nowadays the new arrival is likely to get a company apartment and a list of stores that sell labour-saving gadgets, but the package of benefits includes high pay, often boosted by bonuses based on profits, free housing, six weeks holiday a year, often with a free flight home, and help with children's school fees. The minus side of the equation is that you are living in a city dedicated to work. Hong Kong has limited leisure facilities. Many companies maintain their own boats for employees to use at the weekends: the sea is the only place where you can escape the press of humanity. The expatriate social life is adequate but hardly stimulating. Albert Smith, who visited Hong Kong in 1858, described the young expatriates in the great trading companies as having:

a sad, mind-mouldering time of it . . . I never saw one of the young clerks with a book in his hand. They loaf about the balconies of their houses, or lie in long bamboo chairs, smoke a great deal, play billiards at the club . . . and glance over the local newspapers.

It is not quite that bad now, but no one who comes out to Hong Kong doubts that the principle reason is work.

In return for material benefits the expatriate will be expected to produce results. It is a bargain most find acceptable. David Griffiths, who used to be general manager of the Wembley Stadium, came to Hong Kong to run a new sports complex:

> The name of the game for expatriates out here is they don't tolerate idiots at all; and if you are an idiot or you don't measure up then it is the next plane home and I think that is what probably motivates a lot of expatriates.

For many it is an opportunity too. In Hong Kong promotion is dependent solely on ability not, as is sometimes the case in the United Kingdom, on how long you have been in the job. Ian Thomms, an engineer in his early thirties, is managing the works of a large station under construction for the new Mass Transit Railway; as he points out, back home he would never have had that responsibility at so young an age.

The professionalism of today's expatriate is in part a function of his cost. It is an expensive business employing expatriates, with housing the biggest single factor. In 1982 a two-bedroom apartment in Tsimshatsui at the bottom end of the Kowloon peninsular, and not a high-quality residential area, went at auction for £113,000. To rent a three-bedroomed apartment in Repulse Bay, an area much favoured by expatriates, costs about £3,000 a month. As a result no expatriate can afford to buy; even to rent requires a subsidy from employers. This in turn means that companies with a lot of expatriates on their books find themselves tying up huge quantities of capital in the ownership or rental of property—money which is not earning a profit. The expatriate must earn a return on that money to make it worth the company's while to employ him. Malcolm Gray, a manager with the Hong Kong and Shanghai Bank, estimates that it costs his company two and a half times as much to employ him as a Chinese doing the same job, who would not get the same package of benefits. Asked how long the bank would go on employing him under those conditions, his reply was simple: 'Only while I remain two and a half times as good.'

Many companies in Hong Kong have done their arithmetic and have concluded that the day of the expatriate is coming to an end. Hutchison Whampoa, one of the colony's largest trading companies, employed 200 expatriates in 1975. As part of a deliberate policy the number was reduced to 65 by 1980. Besides considerable financial savings, there was a sound business motive for the move, according to former Hutchison Chief Executive, Bill Wyllie:

The decline in expatriates was inevitable and logical. If 95 per cent of your business is with Chinese customers, you should have Chinese people managing that business for you. I took the view that if we were going to succeed in Hong Kong, we were going to have to create an awareness amongst our Chinese staff that the future of the group was as open to them in terms of advancement as it was to European expatriates.

The expatriate can no longer command a premium on the basis of superior skills. In the past it was 'the expat' who spoke foreign languages, who understood the international markets, who had the management skills and contacts needed for multinational businesses: now more and more Chinese are able to compete on equal terms. The young Chinese entering business today normally has a degree from one of Hong Kong's three universities and polytechnics or from a college in Britain, the United States or Canada; and an increasing number have postgraduate qualifications in management from Stanford, the Massachusetts Institute of Technology or Harvard.

The same is true of Chinese businesses in Hong Kong. A decade ago few people would have been able to name more than a handful of Chinese run companies. The visible part of the economy, the trading part, was run by the great British merchant houses whose names were synonymous with Hong Kong. Hong Kong's business world was dominated by the great Hongs—Swires, Hutchison Whampoa, Wheelock Marden, the Hong Kong and Shanghai Bank, Hong Kong Land and, most famous of all, the 'Princely Hong', Jardine Matheson. For years these companies ruled the roost, carving up the business world between them, and providing Hong Kong with its leadership at every level.

A recent chairman of Jardine's when describing the company, said, 'We are just grocers.' It was a modest way of characterising a company that is older than the colony and has been linked with Hong Kong since the earliest days. From being the biggest opium dealers on the China coast, Jardine Matheson has branched out into a wide range of businesses, including grocery. It is now a multinational conglomerate with activities in twenty countries as far apart as the United States and South America, the Middle East and Britain. In Hong Kong it imports everything from marmalade to Mercedes Benz cars; world wide its interests include sugar refining, engineering, construction, distribution, shipping, air transport, insurance, merchant banking, money broking, timber, property and hotels. It is an impressive range but possibly too diverse: 'I wish I knew what the hell Jardine's does,' commented one of the company's senior managers, 'We seem to do far too many things not very well.' Jardine's growth has been somewhat arbitrary, and many wonder if there is any strategy behind its expansion into so many fields. In business terms it has become a classic conglomerate, the theory being that the very diversity of a conglomerate produces more strength than a single-product company. In Jardine's case some parts of the business—like sugar refining in Hawaii—have failed to make money and have drained cash from profitable parts of the business. As a result, Jardine's overall profits, though good by British standards,

Superli

Hong Kong does everything to extremes. It makes money to extremes and throws up extreme characters. Li Ka Shing is one example. Almost unknown outside the Far East, Li is one of the world's richest men, worth, at one conservative estimate, £500 million. Unlike many of the world's super-rich, he didn't inherit a cent. Born of a peasant family in China in 1924, he came to Hong Kong in 1940—hardly the best time to begin a new life. He started his first business venture in the 1950s and chose one of the classic Hong Kong small businesses—making plastic flowers. He prospered, and launched his property company in 1972.

He named his company Cheung Kong—meaning Mighty River. Now, after Hong Kong Land, Cheung Kong is the colony's foremost property company. The papers in Hong Kong have nicknamed Li Ka Shing 'Superli' and he delights in cartoons which show a bespectacled Chinese Superman leaping from skyscraper to skyscraper. His rise to fame and fortune has been phenomenal and many wonder how long he can keep going at the same pace. Rivals claim he is a one-man band who will burn out: one British company chairman in Hong Kong remarked: 'If I fell under a bus in Central, it probably wouldn't do this company any harm; if Li did, his company would collapse. There's no one who could take over the reins.'

So far Li shows no signs of faltering. Part of his mystique is his supposed link with the People's Republic of China, who seek his advice on investment matters. It is even rumoured, though with no visible evidence, that he is backed with mainland Chinese money. He denies it and says he has complete confidence in the future of Hong Kong:

> I am sure Peking wants it to continue the way it is . . . You want to see my confidence? Look at this building we're sitting in—it's a skyscraper in the heart of town. Well I own half of it—me personally that is; and it's the most expensive property in the world. That's confidence.

But sceptics note that Li has prudently given vast amounts of money to charitable activities in China. That's called taking out insurance and even the richest need that.

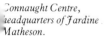

Connaught Centre, headquarters of Jardine Matheson.

have been indifferent by Hong Kong's more demanding requirements. The Princely Hong has been overtaken by newer, more aggressive Chinese companies.

Li Ka Shing, victor in the Battle of the Hongs.

In the mid 1970s new names came to the fore in Hong Kong's business world. They were Chinese companies, generally run by one entrepreneur with great managerial and financial skills. The deliberate low profile of traditional Chinese business was dropped as the real financial strength of these companies became apparent. Two individuals in particular came to prominence: Li Ka Shing, whose Cheung Kong Holdings is now Hong Kong's second largest property company; and Sir Yeu Kong Pao, a Shanghainese banker who had gone into the shipping business after fleeing from China to Hong Kong in 1949. Today, after a series of astute investments in supertankers in the 1950s and 1960s, Pao's Worldwide Shipping Group is one of the largest owners of ships in the world. Both Li and Pao have become immensely rich through maintaining a controlling shareholding in their companies, and, in the late 1970s, the two men formed the spearhead of a challenge to the traditional trading supremacy of Hong Kong's British companies.

Journalists nicknamed the fight 'The Battle of the Hongs' and the complex financial manoeuverings of the last few years are a sign of how the balance of power in Hong Kong's business world is changing. In a series of bids and deals Li took over one of the British Hongs and, with Pao, came close to challenging the mighty Jardine's. The archaically named Hong

Kong and Kowloon Wharf and Godown Company was Li and Pao's first target. As its name suggests it had originally been a wharfage company. In the normal course of business it had acquired a certain amount of property in the Kowloon peninsular. This property was valued in the company's books at its old purchase price and Li saw a classic financial opportunity in the gap between the property's book value and its real market value. The shares were undervalued in terms of the company's real assets. Jardine Matheson owned a small shareholding in Kowloon Wharf and had always regarded it as one of their satellite companies—under the Jardine umbrella as it were. A takeover of Kowloon Wharf would be seen as a direct challenge to Jardine's. In 1978 Li built up a strategic stake in the company—once it was known he was interested the shares took off in value. Li decided to settle for a big profit and sold the shares on to Yeu Kong Pao. Jardine's were visibly shaken at losing a satellite.

Emboldened by the success of the Kowloon Wharf operation, Li looked round for other suitable investment opportunities. Inevitably he looked to one of the Hongs. Swire's and Wheelock Marden were out of reach because of complicated family shareholdings which could not be bought; and taking on Jardine's directly was too ambitious. Li decided to go for Hutchison Whampoa.

Hutchison was the weakest of the Hongs. Its share price was low and undervalued the company. This was as a result of poor trading results in the mid-1970s. Hutchison's had brought in Bill Wyllie, a talented Australian entrepreneur, as chief executive to rescue the company in 1975. Wyllie is one of Hong Kong's most extraordinary characters; a former racing driver, he went into property in the slump of the 1960s when the streets of Hong Kong were taken over by rioters. The market had collapsed but for those with an eye to a bargain, it was the ideal time to buy. He made a fortune when the market revived and in the next few years made a reputation as the colony's toughest company doctor. 'Once a Chinese reporter said to me, "Mr Wyllie, the Chinese say you are a very lucky person." I said, "Yes, that's true; I've noticed the harder I work, the luckier I get".' Nicknamed Dollar Bill for his talent at making money, Wyllie had managed to revive Hutchison's fortunes by the beginning of 1979. The share price of the company had not, however, responded to the better profits Wyllie was producing.

In the autumn of 1979 Li persuaded the Hong Kong and Shanghai Bank, which had a 22 per cent stake in Hutchison's, to sell. The bank sold its shares to Li for HK$7.10 each, a price that was above the existing stock market valuation, but probably below the real value of the company. Within a year the shares were changing hands at HK$20 each and Li had got another bargain. His capital gain on the whole deal was estimated at over £100 million. This time though he was not going to sell out and take his profit.

The man who was most surprised—and angry—at the deal was Bill Wyllie. It wasn't the takeover that he objected to, it was the price. He felt the bank had undervalued Hutchison's and said so loudly. He soon left the company and set up in business again on his own. His view of the takeover was a lot more philosophical than many in Hong Kong; while some saw it as an affront to the British, Wyllie regarded Li's move as 'just another deal'. He explained it to his fellow board members with a simple Darwinian analogy:

> I recall at the time I drew a rough sketch of a fish swimming along—and wrote on it 'China Provident Company', which we were trying to take over at the time. Then I drew a bigger fish behind it with its mouth open, and on that I wrote 'Hutchison Whampoa'; and behind that I drew an even bigger fish and wrote on that 'Cheung Kong', Li's company. That seemed to me to sum it up pretty well.

Others were not so phlegmatic. Jardine's in particular reasoned that if Li was strong enough to take over Hutchison's, they could be his next target. David Newbigging, chairman of Jardine's, mobilised an extraordinary defence. He made a lightning alliance with another of the great Hongs, Hong Kong Land, which involved the two companies swapping a huge number of shares, so that they ended up, effectively, controlling each other. Among the business community it was seen as a desperate move, but Newbigging defends it:

> I certainly wouldn't say it was an act of desperation. Many people said it was a pretty sporting effort. If you bear in mind that over one weekend Jardine's raised the equivalent of four hundred million pounds sterling, over half of which was invested on the stock market between 10 o'clock and 4 o'clock on the Monday, as a result of which we ended up controlling 40 per cent of Hong Kong Land, I would have said that was anything but an act of desperation. Desperate men don't act like that.

The two companies were now locked together in an embrace which meant no one else could take either company over. Trevor Bedford of Hong Kong Land is honest about the reasoning behind it: 'There's no doubt about it that the shareholding in Jardine's was to a certain extent defensive.' Hong Kong Land, a cash-rich property company, didn't find the deal a strain; it could afford it. But for Jardine's the price of the share deal has been high: its balance sheet is now burdened with a very high level of debt. Fighting off Li and Pao has cost Jardine's a lot of money—money that could have been put to better use by investment in the business.

The interesting thing about the battle is that at no stage did Li and Pao actually say they wanted to take over Jardine's. The fear that they might be going to do that was sufficient to force the Princely Hong into an expensive defence. Li did build up a 10 per cent stake in Jardine's—for 'investment' as he put it. In a neat move the shares were sold to Hong Kong Land at a hefty premium, almost two-thirds higher than their market value. It is a measure of the change in the balance of power that today Li's and Pao's every move is studied minutely by the markets and the old Hongs. The moral too has been learnt. Trevor Bedford explains:

The way that companies operated in the old days is not the Hong Kong of today. I just regard Hong Kong as being a very tough, efficient, commercial environment and it doesn't matter what the ethnic base of the company is. Those companies that have changed hands happen to be the old companies. They've done so for the simple reason that they were not operating efficiently in the marketplace.

Others wonder if there is still a place for the traditional British trading companies: journalist Philip Bowring thinks they are leftovers from an earlier age:

> They may have been in control of things in the 1850s. Then they had a real purpose as a link between government and business and as entities which linked the trading, manufacturing and financial sectors. But the economy has now changed out of all recognition and the balance of power has changed. Today the Hongs really are anachronisms.

Those companies which have managed to adapt to the new conditions in the marketplace have survived and prospered, whether British or Chinese. The Hong Kong and Shanghai Bank is a classic example. Once a venerable, rather conservative British-style bank nicknamed 'the Honkers and Shankers' by expatriates, it has reacted to the changes in the economy by backing winners like Li and Pao. Both were financed by the bank in their early years and are now members of the board—Sir Y. K. Pao is deputy chairman. The traditionalists in the British community were outraged that the bank should have sold its stake in Hutchison to an upstart Chinese. The bank regarded it as just another business deal: the only colour it is concerned with is the colour of your money. Chairman Michael Sandberg rams the point home:

> The suggestion that we favour Chinese vis-à-vis British interests is absolute rubbish. I wouldn't say that British influence in the commercial world was slipping away. What I would say is that the local Chinese businessmen's influence has increased enormously. This is a Sino-British mercantile community, and it is that partnership and sense of trust between the Chinese and the British which has been so responsible for the success of Hong Kong.

The bank dominates the business world. With more branches than anyone else in Hong Kong, it alone holds half the colony's total bank deposits. Another one-third is held by associate banks. In terms of stock market capitalisation, the Hong Kong and Shanghai is the most valuable bank in the world; in net income terms it is ranked number fourteen. It has expanded rapidly from its Hong Kong base, taking over the world's twelfth largest bank, Marine Midland of America, three years ago. In April 1981 it tried to take over the Royal Bank of Scotland with a bid worth £500 million. The Monopolies Commission stopped the bid, but the bank is reputedly still in a buying mood. And there are plenty of successful British businesses in Hong Kong.

The Sky-high Man

The invitation is beautifully etched on card: 'Mr and Mrs M. G. R. Sandberg request the pleasure of your company . . .' It's an invitation to a day at the races and is one of the most prized pieces of paper in Hong Kong—far more valuable to the recipient than the notes Mr Sandberg's bank issues. The chairman of the Hong Kong and Shanghai Bank's box at the races is the social and economic pinnacle of Hong Kong society, the invitation a sign that you have arrived.

The old joke about Hong Kong used to be that it was run by the Jockey Club, Jardine's, the Hong Kong and Shanghai Bank and the governor—in that order. Michael Sandberg is chairman of the Jockey Club stewards, banker to Jardine's, chairman of the bank and a member of the Executive Council, the 'Cabinet' which runs Hong Kong. Appropriately, his house is perched on top of the Peak—it's called 'Sky High'. But he's very self-effacing about his position. When asked what it feels like to be the most powerful man in Hong Kong and possibly the world's most powerful banker, he grins: 'I wish it were true. I must tell my directors that—perhaps they'll give me a rise in salary.'

Sandberg started off life as an officer in the 6th Lancers, an Indian Army cavalry regiment. He joined the bank in 1949 and became its executive director ten years ago. Since then he has piloted the Hong Kong and Shanghai into its present position as one of the world's megabanks. He's done it by adapting what was once a typically British colonial bank, all stuffiness and siestas, to the demands of the modern world. He is anything but the fussy, pompous type normally associated with banking and finds irksome the traditional image of a banker as a man who says no: 'A banker has a very rewarding life here. People come to see you with literally little more than an idea in their heads, and you finance them, and years later they are the proprietors of factories employing thousands of people.' Michael Sandberg exudes the sort of self-confidence the British ruling class used to have; the confidence of being born to rule, of being top dog because you deserved to be. Unlike many of his fellow ex-Indian Army officers, now sniffing pink gins in genteel retirement, Sandberg is still a top dog.

Michael Sandberg, Hong Kong and Shanghai Bank.

Aside from the Hong Kong and Shanghai, the second largest bank in the colony, the Standard and Chartered, is British, the biggest property company is British and most of the utilities are British. Britain has the largest share of overseas investment in Hong Kong. But little of it is recent: most of the British companies in Hong Kong have been here for a long time. It is one of the laments of Hong Kong's government that there is so little new British investment in the colony. Although in the financial sector a number of firms have moved in in recent years, few industrial companies have come. According to Bill Dorward, Director of Trade, they are missing a chance:

> I think a lot of opportunities exist for British industry to capitalise on its research skills in association with our people here in Hong Kong. They can come to Asia and fight the competition in its own backyard if they set up factories here in joint venture with our entrepreneurs. That doesn't involve exporting jobs from Britain—what we're talking about is British firms setting up here in joint ventures, cracking markets they otherwise wouldn't have a snowball in hell's chance of getting into.

Using Hong Kong as a sort of foothold within the enemy's camp hasn't caught on in Britain. Yet there are real benefits to those who do so. Thorn EMI, for example, are making TV sets in Hong Kong to sell throughout Asia. Two years ago, Thorn had perfected the TX 9 technology for TV sets. It was an enormous improvement on existing technologies, being more reliable, easier to make and cheaper on energy. It was clearly a major step forward, but Thorn's problem was that complete TV sets couldn't be made in the UK and then shipped to the Far East at a price that would be competitive in the market.

So Thorn went into a joint venture with a Hong Kong electronics company called Promotor. Managing Director Raymond Koo, met one of Thorn's representatives in March 1980 as he was passing through Hong Kong. Koo was keen to do business; he needed a new product line for his factories, and knew Thorn's technology was good: 'We prefer to do business with Thorn, because we have a mutual understanding, a respect for each other.' At the same time Koo was holding talks with a Japanese firm who wanted him to make their product. He was not impressed by them; doing business with the Japanese is, he says, a very slow affair: 'I can't sign a deal with them until they have spent a year finding out who my grandfather is and so on.' By contrast the deal with Thorn was tied up in one month.

Under the terms of the agreement, Thorn's plant at Gosport in Hampshire makes and ships printed circuit boards—the brains of the new TV technology—to Promotor in Hong Kong, who fit them into cabinets and market them. The boards cost about £20 each and Thorn are shipping 25,000 a year at the moment. That means half a million pounds worth of export business for Thorn (plus a percentage royalty on each sale) with none of the problems of marketing and sales back up. It is also a good deal for Mr Koo: he gets a reliable and well-designed product that he can adapt to local market conditions.

Deals like that are few and far between. Most British companies still believe—mistakenly—that they can crack the Asian market from ten thousand miles away. Hong Kong's value to Britain in the future will be as a well-equipped local trading office in the heart of a fast growing market. Sadly it is an office that is little used, says Jimmy McGregor of the Hong Kong Chamber of Commerce:

> British attention has been directed very heavily towards the Common Market and the United States of America. That has meant British companies have missed tricks. We have had heavy attention from the Americans, the Japanese, the Australians, but not from Britain. It's strange because there's a great liking for Britain and British goods here, there's any amount of goodwill. Why doesn't Britain make use of that?

Above: the lion dance, bringing good luck to a new bank branch; below: night-time market; overleaf: Aberbeen Harbour.

CHAPTER TEN

CHINATOWN

The strangest and eeriest place in Hong Kong must be the Tung Wah Coffin Home. It is not a place that visitors to Hong Kong would think of going to see, nor is it on any of the tourist itineraries. But it contains the key to understanding much about the Chinese who make up 98 per cent of Hong Kong's population. It is not a cemetery or a crematorium—both those are final resting places for the dead. It is precisely as its name suggests, a home for coffins. Hundreds of corpses are stored there, awaiting burial. They are the bodies of overseas Chinese from Hong Kong and elsewhere, and their final destination for burial is China. At least that is the theory. In practice, they have to stay in Hong Kong, in many cases for decades, as the Chinese authorities have not so far allowed the coffins to be brought back into China. Like many temporary institutions in Hong Kong, the coffin home seems to have become permanent.

It is a visible sign of the deeply rooted link between the Chinese, wherever they are, and their homeland. Even though in life the residents of Tung Wah chose to live outside China, in death their sincerest wish is to be reunited with their country. The link remains strong even though many of them have never been to China. They have spent all their lives in the Chinese settlements of South East Asia or in the flourishing communities of the United States, Canada, Britain and a dozen other countries. They may have lived all their lives as Chinese Americans, or as British Chinese—but at the end they will always revert to being Chinese Chinese.

For those living in Hong Kong, the dilemma of the relationship with the homeland is sharper. They are closer to China physically and know they depend for their future on China, and Chinese goodwill. Yet many of them have made the conscious and often arduous effort to escape from their homeland. They have settled in a place which is dependent for its very success on its links with the Western world and its adoption of Western industrial and business methods. There is a sharp conflict between the sense of Chineseness and the sense of being separated from China which makes itself felt in every Hong Konger.

For those who were born and brought up in China, the conflict of loyalties is resolvable within traditional Chinese culture and ethics. Just under half the population of Hong Kong—a proportion that is now falling as controls over immigration tighten—was born in mainland China and came to Hong Kong as refugees. For them China is and always will be the homeland, however reluctant they are to live there. And they have faced the misfortunes which decanted them into Hong Kong with equanimity. An early observer of China, Thomas Taylor Meadows, writing in 1847, praised the quality of fortitude which has given the Chinese the strength to overcome difficulties:

> That quality of mind that enables a man to bear pain or adversity without murmuring, depression or despondency . . . to meet danger with readiness and courage . . . any unavoidable evil they regard full in the face . . . almost with a degree of cheerfulness. Every man is induced to learn himself, and to infuse into the minds of his children, a set of doctrines, all inculcating the duty of patient endurance, the necessity of subordination, and the beauty of a quite orderly life.

In essence these are the qualities that have made modern Hong Kong. Re-establishing harmony after it has been broken by events outside one's control is a sacred duty under Confucian ethics. A deep-seated belief in the sacredness of the family institution and the duty of its members to support one another, has been an enormous strength to each immigrant crossing the border in search of a new life. No one coming to Hong Kong came to an alien and friendless land—there were always family members willing to give shelter and food. The links are still two-way for the immigrants in Hong Kong: though few ever wish to return to China to live, many go back on visits. Hundreds of thousands of Hong Kongers cross the border into China every Chinese New Year to celebrate with their families who have stayed behind.

These attitudes have ensured that the assimilation of millions of immigrants has not become the problem it is elsewhere in the world. The immigrants' outlook on life has helped to establish a stable and prosperous society. Starting in many cases with nothing, they were content with whatever Hong Kong could give them, or they could get by their own efforts. They were prepared to work very hard, at all hours of day and night to better the position of themselves and their families. They expected little and their simple expectations were more than met. Their view of Hong Kong was very simply summed up by a Chinese member of the Legislative Council: 'Hong Kong is the lifeboat. China is the sea. Those who have climbed into the lifeboat naturally don't want to rock it.' The ethics of the immigrants made them socially and politically conservative, reluctant to demand anything of government except the right to be left alone. Explained one young Hong Konger:

> My father is a very typical example of the refugee type . . . He came to Hong Kong in his twenties during the war. He was brought up in a very strict set of Confucian ethics, where you do not challenge authority and power. His generation say, if this is the way things are going to be, so be it, let's not say anything.

Chinese peasant en route to shop in Hong Kong.

The attitude that one should accept that events are beyond the individual's control was still strong a decade ago. In a survey for the Chinese University of Hong Kong in 1971, residents of Kwun Tong, an area of Kowloon, were asked if they thought they could do anything to influence government policy: only 14 per cent said yes. Comparable surveys in Britain and the United States have shown that three-quarters of those questioned feel they can alter government policy. Of course Britons and Americans can elect their own government, which Hong Kongers can't; but even so the immigrant generation seems to have had little desire to involve itself in politics even when offered the chance. Of those elected to the Urban Council in Hong Kong between 1951 and 1973, one-third were expatriates—a group making up only 2 per cent of the population. Similarly, until recently only a very small number of people bothered to register for votes in local elections.

But the immigrants are fast becoming a minority in Hong Kong. Tight immigration control has ensured that an ever larger proportion of the population is Hong Kong born and bred and the greatest number of people are now in the fifteen to thirty age bracket. This new generation has very different attitudes; a fact starkly pointed up by the way they dress. On the streets of Hong Kong older people can still be seen in traditional Chinese dress—high button-up jackets, and loose-fitting, square-cut trousers, with the hair worn in a long queue at the back of the neck. By contrast the young native Hong Konger wears Westernised clothes—jeans, T-shirts and sneakers. This new generation has no direct knowledge of China or of traditional Chinese customs, beyond what they have learnt from their parents. Theirs is a different set of values and a different way of seeing the world, and they are beginning to lose the reverence for the elder members of the family that traditional ways demand. They have economic independence and often find the weight of family expectation irksome. For women, expected in Chinese society to remain in the home until they marry and then to produce children, the generation gap has been widest. In the meritocracy of Hong Kong, more and more women are finding it possible to get good jobs with career prospects. Gloria Law, a young Hong Konger in her twenties, gave her family a shock by starting her own business. Then she decided to leave home and get a place of her own. That was regarded as scandalous by her parents because she was not married:

> Chinese people like their children to live with them. Everyone together, you know. My parents were angry with me because I have my own business and I don't give them the money I earn. That's why I have no choice but to leave them and live by myself now.

She was lucky; with the money from her business she could afford a tiny apartment of her own. But the rift with the family will be difficult to repair: 'I want to take care of my parents, but not live with them. Just take care of them occasionally.'

In casting off the constraints of traditional Chinese thinking, many of the more thoughtful young Hong Kongers are conscious that they have lost

Iron in the Flowers

'They're like a rod of iron wrapped up in flowers,' comments Richard Hughes, doyen of Hong Kong's journalists and long-time observer of China and Chinese customs. The Western image of Chinese women is of a demure smiling beauty in a cheongsam, the tight, slit Chinese skirt. Like all images, it is somewhat inaccurate. Traditionally the woman was almost unseen in Chinese society but wielded enormous power behind the scenes. They used to say half of heaven was held up by women.

In today's Hong Kong women are taking a more and more active role in business and public affairs. The prejudice that exists in the British commercial world against women does not exist in Hong Kong. One of the most powerful figures in the colony, Lydia Dunn, is proof of that. Besides running her own highly successful textile firm, she is a board member of one of the colony's most illustrious trading companies, Swire's, and on so many other business boards and semi-official public bodies that her daily schedule is precisely sliced up into minutes allocated here and minutes there. The Legislative Council, the Financial Committee of Legco, the Public Accounts Committee, the Textiles Advisory Board, the Fish Marketing Advisory Board, the Special Committee on Land Production, the Yau Ma Tai Public Square Management Committee and many more public bodies claim her time. She is no token woman either. Besides her active role in business and politics, she has played a major role in the battle to keep the textile industry free of restrictions.

Lydia Dunn is a real Hong Konger—the product of the meeting of East and West. Born in Hong Kong, her parents were refugees. She was educated at the University of California and returned to Hong Kong to work. Like many here, she is determined that Hong Kong is and will be her home, that it must have a future. 'I can't say I have any personal feelings about China. My parents came from there, but it means nothing to me.'

Lydia Dunn, Hong Kong's most successful businesswoman.

something; even the material success attained by some has not altered that. Tsim Tak Lung, a successful young banker in his thirties, who was voted an 'Outstanding Young Person of Hong Kong' by a magazine in 1980, is a good example of the cultural cross-currents of the modern Hong Kong professional class. A graduate of the Hong Kong University, he took a further degree at Manchester University in Britain and then worked for four years with the BBC's External Services in London. He returned to Hong Kong in 1976, well qualified, but somewhat confused:

> The sense of aesthetics I've acquired is foreign not Chinese. The music I listen to and the movies I see are foreign not Chinese. I am painfully aware of the fact that in the world I live in the centres of change are London, Paris and New York. They set the trends . . . we get everything second hand.

The sense of Hong Kong as an imitative society, always following where others lead and without a cultural base of its own, leaves him very unhappy:

> Cultural imperialism bothers me. I believe there is a lot of resentment against this sort of thing among educated Chinese. I can see the advantages of being Westernised but this must not be at the expense of one's own dignity.

124

The resentment against Western influences is often expressed. One graduate, returning to Hong Kong to look for a job after several years of education in Britain, found herself re-learning Chinese in an attempt to fit in again. She was what is cruelly known by Hong Kong Chinese as a 'banana'—yellow skinned on the surface but white underneath. Others try and find ways of retaining their Chineseness. Perry Luk, a chartered accountant with one of the biggest British accountancy firms, runs a Kung Fu club. It isn't just the physical fitness involved in martial arts that interests him, it's the Chineseness of it: 'It is a sort of traditional Chinese art, and we Chinese should keep it on, because otherwise it will disappear.'

For the professional classes like Perry Luk the culture crunch is particularly noticeable: they have had to acquire Western skills in order to compete in a Western oriented world. But the conflict is also apparent further down the social scale. There the reaction to the strange cultural displacement involved in being a Hong Kong Chinese has been a retreat into negativism. Fung Ho Lap, who directs a group of social workers, detects a worrying attitude among Hong Kong's teenagers:

> Many of them are shrewd but they have no positive social values. They have no respect for authority, but won't take sides in any social debate. Such attitudes are a mixture of the worst of Western individualism and the Chinese tradition of not bothering about anyone else's problems.

He feels that the fault lies in an educational system that is unsure of itself and its values. Education in Hong Kong is, like so much else in the colony, a mix of Western and Eastern influences. In its attempts to teach deductive logic, it makes use of the Western tradition of questioning the teacher and received wisdom, but overlayed onto this is the traditional Chinese method of learning by rote. In large measure this is a necessity given the complexities of the Chinese language. As Dr Gordon Redding of the Hong Kong University explains, learning Chinese is fiendishly difficult: 'Without an alphabet or a standardised graphic representation of sound, mastery of the Chinese language involves a formidable test of memory . . . as a person cannot be literate without being able to recall thousands of characters.' In Hong Kong schools, learning by rote is also applied to the teaching of English. The method used is the constant repetition of chosen phrases, making a lot of use of visual symbols. Thus a class will be shown a picture of a melon and asked, in English, 'Is this a lemon?' The reply must be correctly phrased: 'No it is not, it is a melon.' The child will be required to repeat the phrase until perfect. The effect is alarming. Those who have learned English locally speak it with the careful deliberation of people who know something off by heart, but have no idea what it means. It makes conversations in shops and restaurants unnerving for someone who speaks English naturally, but it is a result of traditional Chinese methods of teaching.

Yet these children are brought up in the belief that if they want to get on in life they must speak English. It is the language of government and

business and in a place as dependent on foreign trade as Hong Kong, the inability to speak English is a bar to promotion.

Better than jogging . . . office workers limbering up for the day with Tai Chi.

There are those who resist the pressure to Westernise. Like the young banker Tsim Tak Lung, many Hong Kong Chinese are worried that they are losing contact with their own culture. Lau Chin Shek, director of the Christian Industrial Committee, has deliberately refused to learn English. He knows that it is the passport to social status and acceptability in Hong Kong; a passport that will ensure his views are listened to in government and would give him a place on the numerous government consultative committees. He has refused to learn English because he wishes to show that his loyalties and connections still lie with the vast mass of Hong Kong's underprivileged, most of whom do not speak the language.

The Western-educated young middle class have embraced the English language and the culture that goes with it more readily. But recent actions by the British government have made them wonder if they belong with the West any more than they belong with the Chinese culture of their parents. For two decades now, the bright Hong Kong student has tried to get a university place in Britain if at all possible; the admiration for things British, especially our educational system, is strong. This confidence in Britain was rudely shaken in September 1980 when the government introduced large increases in fees for foreign students at British universities. Despite requests that Hong Kongers be treated as 'home' students, and thus be excused the increase, Whitehall refused to change its mind. The effect was dramatic: whereas in 1979 4,648 Hong Kongers were studying at British universities, in 1981 there were less than half that number. Embarrassed at Britain's action, in 1981 the Hong Kong government started a loan fund which aimed to meet the difference in fees between Britain and other countries and thus ensure a continuing flow of Hong Kong students to British universities.

The episode left a nasty taste in the mouth of many Hong Kongers. It gave them the sense of being rejected by a country they had been brought up to admire. More seriously it will have an effect in the years to come—in the long term to the detriment of Britain not Hong Kong. The students of today are going to the United States and Canada, where university fees are much more reasonable. They will bring back to Hong Kong a taste for the culture—and the goods—of North America. Britain may have lost one of its most potent sales weapons; an enthusiasm for British products from people who have lived in Britain.

The feelings of alienation from Britain was strengthened by the passing of the Nationality Act through Parliament in 1981. This entailed a redefinition of British citizenship into three categories; it had the effect of making Hong Kongers feel like inferior citizens. On their passports Hong Kongers used to have the words, 'Citizen of the United Kingdom and Colonies'. Under the terms of the Nationality Act this was replaced with the words, 'Citizen of British Dependent Territories'. In practice the Act changed little, as British ministers were at pains to point out. The 1971 Immigration Act had already distinguished between British citizens with a right to live in Britain and those without that right. Hong Kong, together with the rest of the Commonwealth countries, was in the second category. Hong Kongers still have the right to visit the UK without a visa, although in practice many consider it advisable nowadays to get one in order to avoid a difficult passage through British immigration formalities.

The change of title was bitterly resented in Hong Kong. The British government claimed it was intended to give Hong Kongers 'parallel citizenship'; it was supposed to emphasise the Hong Konger's relationship with Hong Kong rather than Britain. The two and a half million people in Hong Kong with British passports did not see it that way. To them it was a calculated snub, yet again a sign that Britain did not, and did not want to, understand the needs of Hong Kongers. 'Psychologically it was a let down,' observed Hong Konger Mike Souza, who is married to an Englishwoman.

> As far as Hong Kong travel to Britain is concerned, things haven't changed. But what about the international community as a whole—do they look at this new thing as a British passport, or don't they? At the moment if you are going to the United States, they'll give you a visa because you've got a British passport. If the Americans look at this and say it's not a British passport, what position are we in then?

What really riles Hong Kongers is they have no intention of moving en masse to Britain and settling there; they accept the restrictions on immigration to Britain and have no desire to change them. What they feel cheated of is some form of definition of their status. 'I'm not quite sure what I can call myself,' says Christine Loh, who campaigned against the Act.

> I can't call myself a Hong Konger like a Singaporean can call herself a Singaporean. Hong Kong doesn't have any nationality. We are neither Chinese nor British. We feel the British government ought to clarify our position if only for the sake of form-filling exercises. We would like to see a distinct and separate citizenship for Hong Kong.

That is a status no British government can ever bestow on Hong Kongers. To give separate citizenship is the first step to acknowledging the separate reality of Hong Kong as a state, which would never be tolerated by China. In the eyes of Britain and China there is a tacit recognition of the real status of Hong Kongers. As Loh puts it, 'we are residents of Chinese territory under British administration'.

The identity crisis of the young Hong Konger is certainly not helped by measures like the Nationality Act. Nearer home, too, they find it difficult to define their relationship to the government which rules over them. Christine Loh is the chairman of a group of young professionals called the Hong Kong Observers, founded in 1975 to 'promote informed discussion of public issues, and through such a process attempt to make the government more responsive to the needs of the people'. A seemingly innocent aim, it provoked from government a reaction bordering on paranoia.

The proliferation of such pressure groups in the mid-1970s caused the government to set up a secret committee to monitor their activities. It was called the Standing Committee of Pressure Groups, or SCOPG for short. The committee's report on the Hong Kong Observers, complete with large stamps on it saying 'Confidential', was leaked to the British journal, the *New Statesman*, in December 1980. The report showed that the Observers had been under scrutiny from Hong Kong's Special Branch, which reported to the committee that 'some members may be genuinely altruistic, aiming mainly to right alleged social injustice, while others may be personally ambitious and merely seeking the limelight with a view to their own future. Still others may have radical political intentions.' However, the policemen concluded reassuringly: 'There is no evidence that either the Chinese communists or the KMT [nationalist supporters of Taiwan] have any influence as a whole.' SCOPG's conclusions on the group's influence noted that it had received 'undue importance and status' as a result of being invited to publish a long series of articles in the *South China Morning Post*, Hong Kong's main English language newspaper. 'There is evidence to show that many educated young Chinese believe that the Observers are doing "a good job".'

It might appear from such a report that the government was facing a serious challenge to its power. The Observers were anything but that. A small group, with only just over fifty members at the time of the SCOPG report, it was the sort of middle-class discussion group you would find by the dozen in every town and village in a country like Britain. Its members were all in their twenties and thirties, well-educated professionals in responsible jobs. Its criticisms of government policy were mild, even bland. 'I think the Hong Kong government has been spoiled for a long time,' comments Christine Loh.

> Local people don't usually voice their discontent about anything so the government can do very much what it likes. But this is changing. Our members were born and bred in Hong Kong, this is the only home we've got. We want to be consulted and to participate in decision making. People have gotten over the stage of wanting to take care of their rice bowls. They want to know why it takes them two hours to travel to work. This place can no longer be run on consensus by a small bunch of colonial civil servants.

It says something for the flexibility of the British rulers of Hong Kong, or possible their insecurity, that today the Observers are an accepted and welcome part of the policy-making process of Hong Kong. What was once spied upon by Special Branch is now regarded by government with pride as a group with civic responsibility. The former governor, Sir Murray MacLehose, waxes lyrical about the Observers:

> They are an extraordinarily responsible body, they set about things with very careful research and give a highly constructive expression of views. If ever I feel depressed about what's happening in Hong Kong, I have a dinner party with young people like these and feel happier about everything. There's no better antidote to depression.

That's the sort of recommendation that would have most pressure groups wondering where they'd gone wrong. In Hong Kong it's a sign that the consensus had been expanded to take a new force into account. Left on the outside that force might become dangerous.

It is also an acknowledgement by the government that times have changed; no longer is it dealing with an unsophisticated refugee population. More issues require attention, more groups need to be accommodated into the political structure. The simplicity of the old days, when a civil servant could say, 'Whoever governs Hong Kong may be forgiven by the people for failing to fulfill social ideas but will never be forgiven for adopting policies that put the economy and the standard of living at risk', are gone. The new generation is not content with a government that fails to deliver on social policies.

In many ways the government regrets the passing of the old days. In the New Territories, the government's district officers used to be known in Chinese, as their mandarin predecessors had been, as 'Fu Mu Kuan', 'father-mother officers'. The old Chinese view of politics as an exercise for the resolution of conflict rather than its creation meant that government was sensitive to the demands of traditional Chinese society. Thus, until very recently, polygamy was legal in Hong Kong in deference to the wishes of many in the Chinese community—there are women still alive in Hong Kong

Local Boy Made Good

If Hong Kong is overwhelmingly a society of immigrants and their children, one group can at least claim to be indigenous. The Hakka Chinese are the original inhabitants of the New Territories. They have seen massive changes: in their lifetimes the New Territories has been transformed from a green land of peasant farmers into a suburb of Hong Kong and Kowloon. Some appear to find the change bemusing; others like David Chan have adapted. He was born and brought up on what used to be the island of Tsing Yi. It was a quiet place, inhabited by a few farmers growing rice. It had no electricity, no running water, no sewerage system and no schools. Chan went to school on the mainland—and he went barefoot. Today Tsing Yi has been joined to the mainland by reclamation works, and industrial estates are springing up all over it. David Chan changed with it. Shortly after leaving school, he was taken on by a property company as an interpreter from Cantonese into Hakka and vice versa. He had to negotiate on the company's behalf with the farmers he had grown up with. It struck him that there was money to be made from this on his own account, so he set up his own development company. Now, aged thirty-five, he is a millionaire with a suite of offices in the Connaught Centre, a Mercedes, two boats and a beautiful house by the seaside— from which he can look over to Tsing Yi where he was born.

The redevelopment of the New Territories has had a dramatic impact on the peasants living there. Overnight many who owned a small slice of land became very wealthy: 'They wanted to show off that they're rich,' remembers Chan,

> so they would go first to the barber's shop and get their hair curled into a new style, then they'd buy a fancy new shirt, then maybe a beautiful car. Some were smart though—they used their money to develop a restaurant somewhere—maybe in Soho.

It is one of the improbable facts of Hong Kong that most of the restaurants in the Chinese district of London—Soho—were paid for out of money made from selling land in the New Territories.

Chan has put some of his wealth back into the New Territories. One of the projects he is backing is a fish farm on a small island near his home which produces fish for the restaurant tables of Hong Kong. Chan has financed the business and provided the technical expertise—his partners are a family of poor farmers, who actually manage it on a day-to-day basis. The split in the profits will be fifty-fifty. As Chan says: 'I got a lot out—why shouldn't I put some back in?'

David Chan, peasant boy turned property tycoon.

who lived their married lives as concubines. In deference to Chinese opinion homosexual acts are still illegal in Hong Kong, long after they have been legalised in England.

But the new generation is not content with gestures of deference towards traditional Chinese thinking. Nor is it satisfied by a successful economic policy. It wants a government that does more and does it better. The failure of the housing programme, the seeming inability to eradicate corruption, inadequate social policies, even the traffic jams that clog Hong Kong's streets, making driving impossible, are all issues on which the government is finding young Hong Kongers have views, especially the educated middle class.

While there seems to be no general desire for more representative government among Hong Kongers at large, they do want a system that works better. The middle class wants a hand in deciding that system and a share in power. In a sense this new middle class is a product of a set of government policies which have worked only too well. The ambitious expansion of higher education, the fast rate of growth of the financial and professional sector of the economy, and the general rise in living standards have combined to produce an articulate and self-confident group who are not content to leave the running of Hong Kong to the British administration and its chosen collaborators among the colony's top businessmen. The government has belatedly recognised this new force and is making efforts to integrate it into the management of Hong Kong. Besides being nice about

them, as in the case of the Observers, government has tried to inveigle the noisiest representatives of middle-class pressure groups onto its advisory boards and committees. It has expanded the opportunity for directly elected positions on the district boards in the hope of attracting middle-class energies into administrative responsibility.

Moving up the hill is a sign of making it in Hong Kong.

It has also tried to give the new middle class a stake in Hong Kong as property owners. The price of housing in Hong Kong is so high that only the very rich or companies can afford to buy even average housing. At the bottom end of the market, the vast mass of people will never live in their own homes and are being housed in government accommodation. The gap in the middle is being filled by a home ownership scheme, started in 1977. Initially it was aimed at people with modest levels of income and was an immense success. So far 15,000 families have been allocated government flats which they can purchase at cost price. Another 45,000 flats are to be built in the next decade to cater for anticipated demand. Plans are now being rushed through to extend the scheme to those on middle-class incomes, most of whom are living in expensive private rented accommodation.

But no matter how hard it tries, in its attempts to meet the aspirations of the Chinese middle class, the government is condemned to failure. Hong Kong cannot possibly repeat the dramatic rise in living standards that turned a refugee community into one of the world's greatest trading nations. Economic growth at that rate cannot be sustained indefinitely no matter what economic policy is followed. Failure to continue such growth will not bother the refugee part of the population: they have lived with upheaval and misery before and can do so again. The born and bred Hong Kongers, who have never known anything other than prosperity and rising living standards, will find it much harder to adapt and much harder to forgive those responsible.

Government will never be able to grant the ultimate ambition of the middle class—a meaningful stake in the administration leading to a representative system of government. That would never be acceptable to China. Nor will it be able to soothe away the fear lying at the back of the minds of intelligent young Hong Kongers like Christine Loh:

> I would very much like to look forward to a future in Hong Kong, and what I fear is that I may not be able to do this. What the people of Hong Kong fear most is that Britain and China will come to some agreement on the future of Hong Kong without consulting the people of Hong Kong at all, and that we will end up with something we don't like. I feel that people in Britain don't quite understand how we in Hong Kong treasure living in a liberal environment.

Government has no way of reassuring people like Christine Loh within the constraints of the secret diplomacy that will decide the future of Hong Kong. It can never help Hong Kongers in their search for an identity that is all their own—perhaps because it believes deep down that Hong Kong does not have an identity. Perhaps that thought is also lurking in the minds of many Hong Kongers as they face the future—does Hong Kong have any meaning by itself, or is it an integral part of China?

CHAPTER ELEVEN

TURNING FULL CIRCLE

Writing in 1957, Chairman Mao Tse Tung addressed himself to the problem of the modernisation of China's economy:

> There are two different attitudes towards learning from others. One is the dogmatic attitude of transplanting everything, whether or not it is suited to our conditions. This is no good. The other attitude is to use our heads and learn those things which suit our conditions, that is absorb whatever experience is useful to us. That is the attitude we should adopt . . . As for imperialist countries, we should unite with their peoples and strive to co-exist peacefully with those countries, do business with them and prevent any possible war, but under no circumstances should we harbour any unrealistic notions about them.

Mao's sentiments would no doubt have been echoed by the group of Western merchants in Shanghai who, in 1865, had proposed building China's first railway line between Shanghai and Woosung. It was, by any criterion, an 'unrealistic notion'. Despite considerable misgivings on the part of the Chinese authorities, the project was eventually approved and the line finished in 1875. It ceased operations almost immediately after a man was killed on the line. The indignant Chinese authorities took over the enterprise and ripped up the track. The rolling stock was left to rust on a beach in Formosa. Those businessmen had made the mistake that many have made in believing that China could be forced to modernise, that it had only to see the benefits of modern technology to want to import them.

It is a lesson that holds true today. The dream of opening up China to foreign trade and influence is still as strong as ever. In the last few years China has welcomed foreign traders as a means of achieving its ambitions for modernisation—the so-called 'Four Modernisations' programme. High-powered trade missions from every country on earth have tramped the four corners of China convinced that there was a pot of gold at the end of the trading rainbow. The warnings of those like Michael Sandberg, chairman of the Hong Kong and Shanghai Bank, who have traded for a long time with the Chinese are ignored:

> We've been in Shanghai all the way through . . . There are a billion people in China, it's an enormous market. But it's not perhaps the

market that everyone thought it was going to be. You shouldn't be saying there's a billion people, think how many bars of Cadbury's chocolate we are going to sell, or bottles of ginger pop.

Yet if Hong Kongers take care to warn others about the chimera of China trading, they too are suffering from a parallel illusion. For them the opening up of China seems to represent the solution to all of Hong Kong's problems. The notion of Hong Kong as China's doorway to the rest of the world, thus guaranteeing its own survival, has gripped Hong Kongers to the total exclusion of other realities. They of all people should know the hazards; China trading has never been easy and has never been the security Hong Kongers now think it to be.

From the time of Marco Polo and his accounts of the fabulous size and wealth of China, Westerners have been under the perpetual illusion that there was a simple key to unlocking the riches of the China market. Marco Polo's description of the court of Kublai Khan—'in respect to the number of subjects, extent of territory and amount of revenue, he surpasses every sovereign that has heretofore been or that now is in the world'—created an image of fantastic riches there for the asking. In fact it is probable that Marco Polo never visited China, that his book was a fantasy. Polo's account gave a tremendous stimulus to the early traders with the East, and the belief that there was a fabulous market to be opened up if only tiresome bureaucratic restrictions could be removed came to dominate the foreign policy of countries like Britain towards China.

It was a conviction that led to three wars with China and the establishment of Hong Kong. After the First Opium War it was frustration with the growth of the China trade that provided the emotional impulse towards further conflict. Following a war which had supposedly liberalised all categories of trade, the only business that flourished in the 1840s and 1850s was the opium trade. It was described as 'the largest commerce of the time in any single commodity' and alone yielded one-third of the revenues of British India. It made the fortunes of many of the European traders so that the Taipans of companies like Jardines could reckon to spend only ten years in the harsh climate of China before retiring to Britain as millionaires. Opium comprised one-third of British exports to China in 1851; and it was far and away the most profitable third. Business in other goods was slow and unprofitable; in the main it comprised raw cotton from India and cotton and woollen goods from the factories of England. The appetite of the Chinese for these goods was small and irregular. Though the British had managed to remove many of the restrictions that existed on their goods by the system of treaty ports, where they and not the Chinese had control, there was no way that people in China as a whole could be forced to buy British goods. As many British exporters to Japan today have discovered, there is such a thing as innate nationalism which can block exports even when the price is right.

The merchants demanded yet more concessions from China in an attempt to stimulate trade. In the 1860s there were calls for more government help in forcing China to open up. *The Times* dismissed such appeals from the merchants: 'The opening of the country is their cry, "progress" is

Selling western goodies to China is the original reason for Hong Kong's existence.

their motto, war is their object,' it declared in a leader of 1870. 'Trade is slack at the present. It is necessary to live and Micawber-like they hope for something to turn up in the general disruption it [war] would inevitably produce.' The government refused to act on behalf of the merchants and the stagnation of trade continued. British exports to China totalled only £9 million in 1872.

The merchants did have logic on their side. As late as 1880 China was still technologically one of the most backward societies in the world. It had not a single railway line after the failure of the Shanghai/Woosung experiment, no telegraph lines, not a single machine-driven cotton spindle. Opinion in China was gradually hardening in favour of some attempt to close the gap between China and the West, but there was still a bitter division between those who wanted contact with the barbarian kept to a minimum and those who saw the benefits of such contact however undesirable it might be. Western gunboat diplomacy within the vicinity of the treaty ports—over which the Chinese government had no authority—caused widespread resentment and frequent riots. Along the coastal strip, where there was extensive contact with foreigners, there was a considerable degree of xenophobia. It was not unjustified—it will be a long time before the Chinese forget the sign in a Shanghai park saying 'no dogs or Chinese'.

The uncomfortable results of China's experience with the West gave the reformers who wished to learn from the barbarian the upper hand. The appalling failure of China's armed forces in battle with the much smaller but better equipped Western armies and navies was a stimulus to change. An official programme of modernisation was started in 1860 called 'yangwu yundong'—the 'foreign matters movement'. Its first target was the creation of a modern Chinese armaments industry. An enthusiast for the modernisation programme, Feng Gui Fen, a scholar who was an adviser to the government, claimed in 1861: 'Only thus will we be able to pacify the empire; only thus can we play a leading role on the globe; and only thus shall we restore our original strength and redeem ourselves from former humiliations.' But resistance to Western ideas was strong in court circles: one scholar denounced the teaching of Western science as unpatriotic:

> In 1860 the barbarians took up arms and rebelled against us. Our capital and its suburb was invaded, our ancestral altar was shaken, our Imperial Palace was burned, and our officials and people were killed or wounded . . . How can we forget this enmity and this humiliation for even a single day? Should we further spread their influence and fan the flame?

The insistence that China could only strengthen itself by learning from the West won the day and the policy of modernisation was extended into the economic area. Encouraged by government, communications were improved, mines opened, factories built and the infrastructure of trade and business expanded—all with Western aid in the form of personnel, technology and capital. Geographically it was not a large-scale operation, being confined to the areas around the ports of South China: the vast mass of rural China was left untouched by any modernisation. Nor was it very profitable or rewarding for Western traders. Although the big trading companies operating on the China coast were still making money from the opium trade, which was not abolished till the early years of the twentieth century, they had decided as a longer term measure to offer their services to the Chinese authorities as intermediaries. The great Hongs like Jardine's saw that their future might lie in providing skills and capital to China. The introduction of railways into China in the 1890s involved Jardine's and the Hong Kong and Shanghai Bank in extensive money-raising operations on behalf of China. Jardine's also managed much of the engineering works. This new venture did not prove particularly profitable and it seemed that the great fortunes made earlier in the century could no longer be matched. The politician G. N. Curzon, writing in 1894, noted, 'Large fortunes are made with difficulty; the merchant princes and magnificent houses of an earlier day have disappeared; . . . men do not now expect fortunes; they are content with competencies.'

The end of the nineteenth century saw a change in the British attitude towards China. No longer were the merchants and politicians keen to use force to open up the country. Now that they had allies in the modernisation movement in government, the emphasis was on strengthening the hand of the reformers and averting the chaos that would follow from further military pressure on China. A spate of popular risings against government all across the country had shown that the political structure of traditional China was

Gate 150

'China trade isn't conducted by people in massive offices with huge overheads, it's a small business at a small business level of operation,' says journalist Philip Bowring. The tiny settlement of Pak Hok Chau, at the extreme western end of the border between Hong Kong and China, seems to bear him out. Comprised of a few huts, surrounded by marshy fish ponds and guarded by a small police post, it is also a trading settlement on a small scale. Every morning the junks come in from China with the tide and moor on the sandbanks beside the river. The gate—number 150 in the border—is opened by a Hong Kong policeman and trading commences. Trucks arrive carrying old deck chairs and used car tyres. These are loaded onto the junks and taken off to China. No one knows what the deck chairs are used for, but apparently the car tyres are converted into sandals. One member of the junk's crew is normally dispatched to the nearest town, ostensibly to buy provisions and goods for the commune from which the junk comes. At about five o'clock he returns, weighed down with clothes, radios, Coca Cola and other consumer goods, all wrapped up in bright red and blue carrier bags.

The policeman who guards the frontier is very relaxed about it. He knows that none of the traders will risk losing his licence by smuggling in illegal immigrants. These people who come across the frontier every day have to carry a baffling number of passes from the relevant Chinese and Hong Kong authorities. They used to be known in military parlance as TBCs—Tolerated Border Crossers. Today they are rather more realistically known as CSs—Chinese Shoppers.

The sheer scale of movement across the border is enormous and growing as contact between China and Hong Kong increases. Last year 7.7 million people passed through the railway crossing point at Lo Wu, compared to only 2.2 million in 1977. That is the equivalent of one and a half times Hong Kong's total population. Going into China most of the passengers are Hong Kongers visiting family; coming the other way, it's mainly people from China seeking to buy or sell in Hong Kong. Whatever happens to the politics of the place, this border flow will go on regardless. Formalities are kept to a minimum and everyone seems to accept that's the way it's going to stay.

shaky, its authority undermined not only by Western incursions but also by a weakening grip on its own people. Further pressure from outside could bring it down.

The weakness of the system of government was clear to many within China as well. After a series of factional battles in the imperial court at the turn of the century, the reformers eventually consolidated their control and embarked on large-scale modernisation of the machinery of government. A decree from the Empress Ci Xi in 1901 declared:

> Up to the present the study of European methods has gone no further than a superficial knowledge of the languages, literature and mechanical arts of the West . . . China has hitherto been content to acquire the rudiments of European language and technicalities, while changing nothing of her ancient habits of inefficiency and corruption. The chief defect of our system of administration is undoubtedly too close an adherence to obsolete methods.

Such a commitment to reform was already too late. The imperial system of government was running out of steam. There were continual uprisings all over China in the last years of the nineteenth century, but the final revolt against the Manchu imperial dynasty broke out in 1911 near Hankow on the Yangtze. It was led by Sun Yat Sen, a revolutionary who had been educated abroad, first in Honolulu where his brother lived, then by British missionaries in Hong Kong. His revolutionary credentials had been established in 1897 when Chinese officials made an attempt to kidnap him in London. The revolution surprised many, including Sun, by achieving swift success. By the end of 1911 province after province had declared independence from Manchu rule in Peking and the government was on the defensive. Imperial power soon collapsed and Sun Yat Sen was sworn in as the first president of the new Chinese Republic on 1 January 1912.

The vision of a new China shared by Sun Yat Sen and the republicans was soon dashed. Within a year Sun had resigned as president and a battle began between the various factions that had made up the revolutionary movement. The breakdown of the central administration of China meant that the new republic was to be in chaos for years to come. Separate parts of China that had long resented central control from Peking went their own way under the control of local warlords. Sun Yat Sen died in 1925 while still engaged in an attempt to reunify China under one government. The party that he had founded, the Nationalist or Koumintang Party, was inherited, together with its army, by Chiang Kai Shek. At the same time there was a splitting of the revolutionary movement as more and more workers, especially in the industrialised areas of the south, joined the newly formed Chinese Communist Party. In the 1920s the two parties remained in uneasy alliance in their struggle to reunite and modernise China. In 1927 Chiang, alarmed at the apparent success of the Communist Party, turned on it and instigated a civil war that was to continue for two decades, interrupted only by a partial alliance against the Japanese. The battle against the invaders united all Chinese from 1937 until the final defeat of the Japanese in 1945. Almost immediately thereafter the alliance between the Kuomintang and the Communists disintegrated and civil war broke out again. It ended with complete victory for the Communist Party, under the leadership of Mao Tse Tung, in 1949.

The near continuous disorder which prevailed in China for forty years meant that the economy—and with it the China trade—was in ruins. Revolution, civil war, foreign invasion, flood and famine had devastated China. Industrial production in 1949 was about half the highest level it had reached before that date. The task facing the new rulers of China was enormous.

The first priority was to restore order and the rule of central government. This was done with surprising speed. Mao's next priority was the redistribution of land from 4 million landlords to 300 million peasants. The first few years of communist rule saw a concentration on land reform and improved food production, and the ability of China to feed itself has been one of communism's major achievements since 1949. By the early 1950s Mao was able to turn his attention to industry. Factories were gradually taken over by the state, although former owners were, in some cases, retained as managers on good salaries. By 1952 61 per cent of industry was in public hands. In 1955 the first economic plan, prepared with the help of the Soviet Union, directed the lion's share of new investment into heavy industry.

The reliance on Russian technology and Russian advice was essential in view of the United Nations ban on trade with China, imposed in 1951 in the wake of China's intervention in the Korean War. No Western nation traded with China. It was a dependence Mao found worrying for it meant China had to follow the Soviet route to development—with its emphasis on heavy industry, strong centralised planning and growing rates prescribed by five year plans. Mao felt such a pattern held China back and in 1958 he attacked Soviet advisers as 'timorous greybeards, wedded to excessively cautious rates of development and lacking confidence in the Chinese people'. He felt that China was in danger of becoming a Russian satellite—70 per cent of trade was with the communist bloc by 1955—and that China had to go her own way. The Soviet Union mistakenly tried to force China into toeing the line in the autumn of 1960 by withdrawing 1,300 industrial advisers—which merely increased Chinese determination to go it alone. The final split came about after a bitter war of words in the autumn of 1962, since when relations between the two communist superpowers have been, at very least, strained.

In 1958 Mao had inaugurated his own style of economic development—the Great Leap Forward. It was an attempt to speed up the transition to communism by devolving development decisions downwards and drawing in the energies of all the people of China. The shortages of materials and skills were to be made up for by enlisting a huge and enthusiastic labour force. But it was not enough to ensure success. The Great Leap Forward failed dismally—poor planning, a demoralised and confused agricultural sector, bottlenecks in transport and supply, a worn-out industrial base—there were too many technical problems to overcome. China ended up with a foreign debt of US $700 million and a string of projects that were never to be completed.

Mao's conclusion about the failure of the Great Leap was that China was lacking in revolutionary fervour rather than in the more mundane essentials for development. As one Shanghainese newspaper put it in 1967:

> Of the thousand and one means of developing socialist production, the most important is to drive ahead vigorously with the revolution on the political and ideological planes. If that action is successful, there will be an increase in the production of cereals, cotton, oil, steel, cast iron and coal. If not it will mean failure.

Mao determined to rekindle China's revolutionary spirit. The failure of the Great Leap Forward had led to a somewhat more conservative economic policy which Mao complainingly denounced as 'taking the capitalist road'. In the summer of 1966, he launched a second revolution with the aid of a new group of revolutionary shock troops—the Red Guards—under the slogan, 'We are the critics of the old world; we are the builders of the new world.' The Cultural Revolution witnessed an assault on conservative thinking throughout the length and breadth of China, in government, the party, the army and the economy. Factories were taken over, managers harangued, museums ransacked, houses looted—and industrial production dropped by 15 per cent to 20 per cent. Eventually the army started taking an active part in politics in an attempt to restore stability. During the Cultural

Revolution China effectively became a closed society again. No visitors were allowed in and the revolution had more than a touch of xenophobia as Red Guards attacked foreign technology as unrevolutionary and un-Chinese.

The return of order at the end of the 1960s meant a new start to the process of building up China's economic power. For the Western traders the Cultural Revolution had almost entirely stopped what little business there was with China. Indeed the revolution had been exported to the streets of Hong Kong, and at one time many in the colony were convinced China intended to take over Hong Kong. The moment passed, and everyone wondered what direction China would pursue next. After a period of internal political upheaval, the 'revisionists' who had been ousted in the Cultural Revolution returned to the saddle, principal among them Deng Xiaoping. He had earned the enmity of the Red Guards by being somewhat too pragmatic during the 1960s; in a famous speech in 1962 he had claimed, 'For the purpose of increasing agricultural production, any by-hook-or-by-crook method can be applied. It doesn't matter whether a cat is black or white as long as it catches mice!' It had been Deng who had helped clear up the economic mess left by the failure of the Great Leap Forward; now he was called on to do the same job again. After Mao's death in September 1976, there was further factional fighting between supporters of Deng and supporters of Mao's widow. Deng won and the Gang of Four—Madame Mao and her allies—were ousted. Deng's economic policy was simply summed up under the title 'Four Modernisations', by which he meant the overhauling of China's antiquated defence, industry, science and technology and agriculture. The aim was still as it had always been—to transform China into the major world power it felt it ought to be.

The Four Modernisations is still the official policy of China, and it has meant the reopening of China for trade on a massive scale. The problems to be faced are massive too. Of China's 800 million peasants, one-third have insufficient incomes—incomes of less than £20 a year—according to China's Minister for Agriculture. Speaking in December 1981, Du Run Sheng reported that the peasants, 'are free from exploitation, but have not yet shaken off poverty'. China's industrial plant is old fashioned, inefficient and in need of replacement. The immediate targets are to give more freedom to peasants so that they can produce goods for sale on their own account; a shift of emphasis away from heavy industry to light industry to meet consumer demand; to improve energy supplies; and to increase the general standard of skills available in Chinese industry. Inevitably this involves the help of outsiders—China does not possess the skills or the technology. The Western world in particular has been invited to participate in the modernisation of China. Within a year of the announcement of the Four Modernisations in 1978, agreements on economic co-operation had been signed with Japan, Britain, France and Italy, and nearly one thousand joint-venture projects were in hand with non-Chinese partners, covering the whole range of the economy. For the first time in China's history, it was China that was asking for trade and technology—China that took the initiative in drawing up the legal arrangements which would facilitate trade. It seemed to a wondering world as if at long last the dream of the China trade was coming true.

Unfortunately, like many shifts in Chinese policy, the Four Modernisations did not take account of reality. By 1980 it was clear that the scale of the projects undertaken was far too ambitious. Most cripplingly, China simply did not have enough foreign exchange to pay for all the goods and equipment it wanted. With the influx of foreign goods, China began to experience inflation for the first time. Following a series of budget deficits, China's inflation rate was estimated to be 15 per cent by mid-1980. Unemployment, supposedly unknown in socialist countries, also became a problem as people moved from the country into the towns. It was clear that the economy was not capable of sustaining the pace of over-rapid modernisation. The brakes were slammed on in 1980. As a result many projects were suspended or indefinitely postponed, like the massive Boashan steel works near Shanghai which, together with various associated schemes, involved an investment of US $2.5 billion.

The abrupt move into reverse gear was a shock for the hordes of Western businessmen who had flooded into China in search of contracts. The halt may be only temporary. China has enormous underlying strength. Unlike most developing countries it is not burdened with foreign debt and believes in taking the pace of development at a rate suitable to the demands of China and no one else. China will not buy anything just because it is modern—a pattern of development which has been adopted for over a century. Internal constraints are important too. Today's rulers have found,

Conveyor belt carrying aggregate across the border.

as the emperor's civil servants found, that the administrative system of China is incapable of working efficiently enough to meet the demands put upon it. Recently a drive has been launched to wipe out corrupt and bureaucratic practices among the government's agencies.

But all observers seem to agree that there is a real future in the China trade, despite the current hiccough. Many companies in Hong Kong see the colony's role in this as China's interface with the rest of the world. Almost all the major companies in Hong Kong have China trading departments, which conduct a lot of Peking's business with the rest of the world. Although Peking has many of its own institutions represented in Hong Kong, like the Bank of China which conducts China's foreign exchange policy and is widely regarded as one of the colony's shrewdest banks, it does not have all the foreign trading skills that have become necessary. Many companies are filling that gap. Fung King Hey, founder of the Sun Hung Kai Bank in Hong Kong, operates as a discreet middleman for China—hunting out skills and technology on behalf of China and then arranging the bureaucratic paperwork on behalf of the Western company involved. Fung describes the job as 'a bridge. We can help bring about effective communication between both parties and bring them to a joint venture agreement.' He admits however that his investment in trade with China is 'long term', which is a polite way of saying it doesn't pay. One of Mr Fung's managers is said to have asked him why the company didn't invest in some real estate in Hong Kong as this would make much more money than China trading: 'Mr Fung

145

said we have to see it in the long term by doing something for the country now.'

After Sun Hung Kai, Jardine Matheson is probably the colony's largest China trader, reverting to its traditional role. But, as chairman David Newbigging readily admits, it isn't very profitable:

> Absolutely true, it isn't. But we want to be there, in the lead. We were the first to have an industrial joint venture there. We've got three offices established in China now. We're taking a medium to long term view of it, both as a matter of the business we might do with China, and hopefully because we want Hong Kong to be perceived in China as being a contributor to their modernisation.

Any opening up of China is good news for Hong Kong. Trade with China is expanding rapidly—in 1981 the growth of imports from China was 34 per cent and of exports to China 82 per cent. Forty per cent of China's foreign exchange earnings come through Hong Kong. In some ways this is highly visible. Without China, Hong Kong would starve. China provides about half of Hong Kong's food, including some 1,000 tons of rice a day. Hong Kong is also China's shopwindow to the world. In the massive China products department stores all over Hong Kong, every conceivable form of consumer product is sold. And they'll take credit cards in payment. On the other side of the coin, as China has opened up, Hong Kong has found its position as a Western office block in China increasingly valuable. Firms wishing to do business with China make Hong Kong their stop en route, and often open an office in the colony so as to benefit from Hong Kong's enormous experience of the China trade. Businessman Raymond Koo, who is now involved in a joint venture with the British company Thorn manufacturing TV sets in Hong Kong from British components, has also introduced Thorn to the Chinese and is opening a further plant, based again on British kits, in China. Koo feels that Hong Kong has a vital role to play interpreting the two sides to each other: 'We are Chinese, we speak the language, we know we think the same way, plus the fact that we have Western training.' But Koo admits it is not easy going: 'The three golden rules of doing business with the Chinese are patience, more patience and most patience.'

China seems to have acknowledged the special position of Hong Kong as a trading partner. Just across the border from Hong Kong, around the town of Shum Zhum, the People's Republic has set up what is known as a Special Economic Zone. In all, 125 square miles of China have been turned into what is in effect an adjunct of Hong Kong. The SEZs (there are others elsewhere, but none have boomed as much as Shum Zhum) are the enterprise zones of China—places where bureaucracy is kept to a minimum, and foreign firms are encouraged to set up plants by offering good tax provisions and generous financial aid. Launched in 1980, Shum Zhum has been transformed from a sleepy border town into one of the fastest growing industrial centres in Asia. Over 700 individual joint-venture projects between Chinese and foreign companies have been agreed so far, involving some £250 million in foreign investment.

Nearly all the production is consumer goods and they are intended for export via Hong Kong to the markets of the world. For China it represents useful foreign exchange and a transfusion of skills and capital. For the foreign joint venturer, China is a remarkably cheap production centre. Most of the factories that have moved there have come from Hong Kong— production costs can be at least a third and as much as a half cheaper than in the colony. The opening up of the SEZ has meant that factories that were becoming uneconomic in Hong Kong due to rising costs can have a new lease of life across the border.

Some have warned that there are risks attached to what amounts to this building of a mini Hong Kong next to the real thing. If China learns how to do it on her own, so the argument runs, it won't need Hong Kong and this new lifeline for the colony could prove a noose round its neck. Already it is estimated that 5,000 jobs in the textile industry in Hong Kong have gone in less than two years. Many of the plants have simply moved across the border to take advantage of China's lower labour costs; it is estimated that the output of 20–30 per cent of Hong Kong's factories could be lost by transfer across the border within five years. The government seems unworried. It has welcomed the SEZ as a sign that China does not have any hostile intentions towards Hong Kong. Bill Dorward, Director of Trade, thinks that losing labour-intensive industries to China is a good thing:

> There's always a shaking out at the bottom of Hong Kong industry. It happens all the time. There's no feather bed, so they just go. Some of the ones at the bottom are now drifting across the border. This strikes me as being quite a healthy development, healthy from China's point of view, healthy from ours. It means that we can then divert our resources into higher technology, more productive industry.

The reopening of the China trade is valuable to the security of Hong Kong, according to Dorward. It has meant the colony's history has now come full circle: 'Hong Kong was founded 140 years ago as an entrepôt, and it's rediscovered that role today. The entrepôt trade, the service sector, is the part of the economy which is growing very fast.' From the business world, David Newbigging is emphatic about the long term benefits: 'There are many compelling reasons, as we see it, for Hong Kong to continue to be very useful to China and thereby to warrant, if you like, special consideration in terms of its future.' The link between the modernisation of China and the security of Hong Kong's future is made by everyone in Hong Kong. So many conversations begin with the phrase 'Of course there'll be no trouble while we are so useful to China . . .'

In one sense the optimism on which this is based is sound. While China needs technology, capital and skills from outside, Hong Kong will obviously play a key role as middleman in that process. In another sense that optimism is based on an unsound reading of China's history. At the moment the China trade is flourishing, and sweetness and light prevails in China's relations with the rest of the world. But as we have seen going right back to

A Foot in Both Camps

In the days leading up to the communist takeover of China in 1949, so the legend runs, the bridge over the Shum Zhum River from China into Hong Kong came close to collapse as Rolls-Royce after Rolls-Royce crossed it, carrying wealthy Chinese to safety in the colony. The weight of the cars was reportedly much increased by the quantities of gold each one carried. Groaning at the axles, they carried entrepreneurs into Hong Kong with the essential commodity that would enable them to start up in business again.

Today the flow has reversed. Many of Hong Kong's rich businessmen take their wealth into China. These days they fly and the wealth is in the more modern form of bankers' drafts and investment schemes. The welcome in China is as warm as the 1949 welcome was in Hong Kong. But one businessman still does it in the old-fashioned way. Alan Lau, an entrepreneur with factories in Hong Kong and China, is driven in his chocolate Rolls-Royce from Kowloon up to the road bridge at Man Kam To where another car picks him up and takes him on a sort of royal progress of the industrial estates of Shum Zhum. Mr Lau's company, Millie's Group, makes a wide range of goods from handbags to shoes on both sides of the border. He is pro-Shum Zhum, but realistic about its benefits. He knows that Hong Kong will soon be too expensive a place to manufacture the sort of cheap consumer goods his company relies upon. Wage costs and the high price of land are forcing Hong Kong out of high-volume, low-value goods, but these are precisely the sort of things China can make—and cheaply. The package Alan Lau has extracted from the Chinese government includes virtually free land, heavily subsidised factories and power, and cheap labour. There is a price—Chinese knowledge of running a business is rudimentary by Western standards, and almost all management has to be imported from Hong Kong. Similarly the quality of Chinese-made products is poor by comparison with those of Hong Kong. The benefits though, outweigh these disadvantages: 'They may know nothing about running businesses,' says Lau, 'but with no rent bills, no power bills and a cheap labour force, I can put up with a lot and still make money.' Enough to pay for a new Rolls-Royce perhaps.

Tourist experiencing China.

the origins of China trading, the history of China has not been one of a steadily maintained course of policy.

The most obvious fact about China is that it does not need trade and contact with the rest of the world. It is to all intents and purposes capable of feeding its own population. It is reluctant to borrow money abroad and pays off foreign debt as soon as possible. It has shown in its space and atomic programmes that it has its own considerable resources of essential scientific skills. Foreign trade is a mere 6 per cent of its gross national product, and there is every sign that China's living standards and internal stability could survive the breaking off of trading contact with the rest of the world. Above all, as the quotation from Chairman Mao at the beginning of this chapter makes clear, China will only remain open to foreign trade as long as it is clearly beneficial to China.

Another factor that mars this glowing scenario of a future for Hong Kong as China's financial and services centre is one which is never mentioned in Hong Kong, the sheer instability of modern China. Much could happen in the fifteen years before the New Territories lease comes up for renewal: during the last fifteen years there has been the Cultural Revolution (which nearly resulted in the collapse of Hong Kong), a period of isolation while China fought over the fate of the Gang of Four, a period of totally open trade and the current period of partially restricted trade. The leadership of China is old and by no means certain of its power base. No communist state has yet found a way in which power can be handed over painlessly and without major changes in the direction of policy—will China be any exception?

Furthermore, liberalisation of the economy has brought its own strains. The introduction of consumer goods into a society that has until recently been starved of such luxuries has produced evils like corruption. Traditional Chinese ethics have been put under strain by policies which seem to have encouraged Western vices. During our filming in Shum Zhum Special Economic Zone, a waiter in a restaurant dared to ask if he could keep the change from the money he was given in payment for the lunch bill. Our Chinese guides were outraged and a major incident ensued. It was reported to Peking and anguished meetings were held with the local authorities to see what should be done about such bourgeois conduct. Yet the unfortunate waiter was only doing what would come naturally to his cousins in Hong Kong. The incident was an indication of the strains imposed by openness on a hitherto closed society. The degree of xenophobia inherent in China is underestimated in the West and Hong Kong. China hates any dependence on others and, as has been seen many times in her history, is quite capable of expressing that hatred in violent and unpredictable forms.

CHAPTER TWELVE

UNDOING HISTORY

Once or twice a week, a discreet little tea ceremony takes place in a nondescript government office block half way up the Peak behind central Hong Kong. The manager of Xinhua, the New China News Agency, comes to consider matters of 'mutual interest' with the political adviser to the governor. Over a cup of Chinese tea they discuss any outstanding problems between Hong Kong and China. Sometimes the topics are important—major new restrictions on immigration for example. Sometimes they are petty; as in one meeting last year in which the Hong Kong government outlined its plans for a clampdown on a phoney driving licence racket. China—in the form of Xinhua—was consulted because it seems that people from Hong Kong, in an attempt to get round the waiting lists for driving tests in the colony, had been slipping across to China, getting a licence quickly and then demanding, back in Hong Kong, that it be honoured as a proper licence. In many cases they had not taken driving tests. The government wished to stamp out the fraud, but would not do so until Peking assured them of its approval. At the next meeting the Xinhua manager was able to tell the political adviser that Peking could see no objections to action being taken.

It was a typical episode. Hong Kong's government knows that everything it does must have the invisible approval of China. Many British officials feel they are in effect managing Hong Kong on behalf of the People's Republic, not Britain or the people of Hong Kong. In 1883 a proposal was made to formalise the curious arrangement now carried out through the tea ceremony. It was suggested in Britain that China be represented in Hong Kong by a consular official. The Hong Kong government refused point blank on the grounds that such an official would become a natural focus for anti-government discontent. The Chinese government of the time was little more enthusiastic. For them such a move represented acceptance of the separate status of Hong Kong.

In formal terms the relationship between Hong Kong and China is conducted through the Foreign Office in London. That department's recent performance over the Falkland Islands crisis has hardly raised the confidence of Hong Kongers that Britain can and will seek a just and lasting settlement to the Hong Kong problem. Everyone realises that if China moves in tomorrow, no one will send a task force to protect Hong Kong. The military option of fighting in defence of historical rights of sovereignty,

as exercised in the Falklands, is neither politically sound nor militarily feasible. The Chinese reaction to the counter invasion of the Falklands showed by its ritual denunciation of imperialist aggression that any such action was out of court. By the same token, no one thinks that China has in mind a military solution. Although there have been times when China has threatened the colony with invasion—and the threats have come both from nationalist and communist governments—it is not regarded now as a plausible option. The army China maintains near the border with Hong Kong is mainly engaged in helping to prevent immigration into Hong Kong becoming uncontrollable. In its spare moments the men are drafted onto construction projects in Shum Zhum.

Not that China would need to invade. World opinion would be overwhelmingly on China's side in the event of any conflict over Hong Kong and the Foreign Office knows this. They also know that the next step is in the hands of China. Over the years, as 1997 and the end of the lease have got closer, successive British ministers have intimated that they would be happy to discuss the matter whenever the Chinese want. So far the Chinese have not indicated they would like to discuss it. The most recent British ministerial visitor to China, former Lord Privy Seal Hymphrey Atkins, came away feeling he had detected a slight movement on the part of China:

> I found the Chinese government recognised the fact first of all that this is not a problem that can be left until the last minute, and secondly that if the particular status and qualities of Hong Kong are to be preserved, the government of China and ourselves and Hong Kong have got to get together to find out what is the best way to go ahead. I think the Chinese are not people who solve everything in five minutes. I know we're not going to get answers this year, but I think we're going to move steadily towards a solution.

Reassuring words, yet they add up to little more than Deng Xiaoping's statement to Hong Kong's former Governor, Sir Murray MacLehose, when he visited Peking in 1979. Deng said that investors in Hong Kong should 'put their hearts and minds at rest'. In the autumn of 1982 Mrs Margaret Thatcher is scheduled to visit Peking; top of her agenda is the future of Hong Kong. It is a reasonable bet that she too will come away disappointed. Although it will be the first visit to China by a serving British Prime Minister, Mrs Thatcher will probably have to be content with fulsome praise for her tough anti-Soviet stance in foreign policy—much admired in China—and some vague generalisations about the future of Hong Kong.

There are two schools of thought about what is going on in the Chinese government's mind. The conspiracy theorists hold that everything has been sorted out and that the Chinese are merely waiting for a suitable time to announce it publicly. The other theory is that the Chinese haven't a clue how to go about grappling with the problem and for the time being are letting the momentum of events decide for them. One ingenious solution, aired in Hong Kong earlier in 1982, ran as follows: Britain would repudiate both the lease and the treaties under which she holds Hong Kong and

Lion outside the Bank of China. China is the lion, Hong Kong the cub.

Kowloon (in theory leased to Britain in perpetuity), and the New Territor
ies would become an extension of the Shum Zhum Special Economic Zone,
ultimately controlled by China but administered by Britain. The story was
strongly denied by the Foreign Office and the Hong Kong government.

The impact of the rumour on Hong Kong was enormous. The Hang
Seng stock exchange index fell 43 points when the denial was issued. It was a
measure of the extent to which confidence is dependent on a peaceful
settlement. The received wisdom in Hong Kong is that with China so
dependent on the colony as a provider of foreign exchange it will be
reluctant to do anything to rock the boat. Officially the line is all optimism,
in an attempt to boost morale and therefore confidence. Sir Murray
MacLehose is bullish about the prospects:

> Tax is at 15 per cent. This is a stable community, it's got a stable fiscal
> environment. It's got one thing that's uncertain, which is its political
> future. So you've got one risk; where else in the world can you say
> there's only one risk?

Sir Murray assesses that one risk as important but by no means overwhelm-
ing. The Chinese view of it, as perceived by him in his discussions with
Chinese officials, is almost abstract and theoretical: 'Their position is that
Hong Kong is part of China, and it is a problem left over from history, and
one day it will be reincorporated into China.' He pauses to emphasise the
word. 'One day, no question particularly of when.'

Not everyone can whistle in the dark as loudly as Sir Murray. The
question of confidence is a real one. Those who remember the last time there
was a run on confidence, during the Red Guard inspired riots of the Cultural
Revolution, are less phlegmatic about it all coming out right in the end. Bill
Wyllie, who went into property during the upheavals of 1967, remembers
how some people in Hong Kong reacted then:

> Confidence is a very fragile thing. When we had the riots and
> disturbances here in Hong Kong, the wealthy Chinese, the people
> who had the mobility and flexibility to do so, left here in droves. They
> went off to the United States and to Canada and established
> businesses, then when things quietened down they came back again.
> Right now people are still confident because 1997 is still a long time'
> away. I believe that 1985 is probably the critical period.

Already there are signs in Hong Kong that people are putting their money
into assets that are mobile or far away from Hong Kong. Thus the gold and
jewellery business is flourishing: many Chinese came into Hong Kong laden
with gold, as a mobile asset, and that's the way they're going to go, if they
have to. Others are investing heavily in ships, which can be based elsewhere
if need be. Yet more are taking advantage of the daily advertisements in
Hong Kong's papers for land in Canada, Australia and America. Having an
asset well out of the reach of a potential communist government is a good
insurance policy.

State Within a State

Walk along Tung Tau Tsuen Street in Kowloon and between the illicit dentists' shops that congregate on the south side of the street can be seen small gaps that appear to lead down to endless darkness. This is the entry to Kowloon's Walled City. The walls have gone now (pulled down during the Japanese occupation of Hong Kong) but otherwise the city has changed little since the first days of British occupation.

The Walled City is, depending on your audience, an integral part of Hong Kong or the last bit of China in the colony. When the New Territories were leased to Britain in 1898, the area of the Walled City was specifically excluded. It was to remain under Chinese jurisdiction. Two days before the British flag was to be hoisted over the New Territories, acquired under the Convention of Peking, the inhabitants of the Walled City rioted against the notion of leasing any of China. The British authorities put down the riot and in reprisal expelled Chinese jurisdiction from the old city. The Chinese government has never accepted this unilateral action, which may explain the Walled City's strange position today.

Effectively it has no administration. The Hong Kong police tend to keep clear of it, and criminals often lose themselves in its rabbit warren of streets. No town planning or public sanitation has ever been undertaken there, with the result that today it is a slum of densely packed apartment blocks. The streets are only three or four feet wide and if you look upwards you can just see the daylight between the buildings fourteen stories up. It is a ramshackle place with facilities like electric power (required during the day to light the streets) pirated from official sources.

More than 50,000 people live in the Walled City, coming out into the streets of Hong Kong for work or shopping. Otherwise it is a self-contained, self-regulating community which doesn't welcome strangers. Visitors to Hong Kong are advised not to enter without a guide. It is living its own life—just as, one suspects, it did before the British arrived. And just as it will continue to do after the British leave.

For the vast majority these options do not exist. If the Chinese take over Hong Kong they will become mainland Chinese again. They don't want that, but they are not sure that Britain, as Hong Kong's sponsoring power, understands the strength of their feelings. There is great fear of Britain doing nothing: a fear that Hong Kong will be allowed to go down the drain through indifference as 1997 approaches and confidence ebbs. Hong Kong's future is not seen as an important issue in British politics. As Bill Wyllie says, it is almost a non-issue: 'A lot of your politicians don't really understand what is going on in Hong Kong. It particularly applies to some of the Labour politicians; some of the statements they've made about Hong Kong demonstrate an abyssmal ignorance.' One paper in Hong Kong has even suggested a remedy, 'a one-week charter tour for the entire House of Commons might turn Hong Kong's relations with Britain inside out'.

Attempts to explain that Hong Kong has real and tangible benefits, while costing Britain almost nothing to run, is the duty of the Hong Kong government office in London. It is a thankless task, and one which yields few dividends. The British government has given its ritualistic support for the continuance of Hong Kong as it is, but has not gone further than that. In part this has been because the British view is, rightly, that the next move is for the Chinese to make; but in part it is a sign of the apathy induced by any parliamentary debate on the future of Hong Kong. No one really wants to know, and no British government wants to stick its neck out by making proposals to China that could form a basis for negotiation.

Border police station, Sha Tau Kok.

The people of Hong Kong wonder if this means that they will get no say in what happens to them. Traditionally Hong Kongers are not terribly interested in what the government does; but on this issue, opinion is mobilising. A recent survey conducted in Hong Kong showed that the vast majority of Hong Kongers are concerned about the lease. Only 1 per cent said they were happy with Peking's current policy of saying nothing beyond vague general assurances; only 11 per cent found Peking's current policy of increasing its investment in Hong Kong comforting (despite the fact that in official circles this is seen as one of the firmest indications that China has no hostile intentions towards Hong Kong). Three-quarters of the sample demanded some positive statement from Peking. The second half of the poll asked what role Hong Kongers should play in deciding their future: 4 per cent were happy to wait and see what happened; 31 per cent demanded a colony-wide opinion poll, with the results sent to London and Peking; while the majority, 54 per cent, wanted to create their own representative bodies so that they could have an organised say in their own future.

The hope in London and Peking that the matter can be settled quietly is vanishing. Of course the exact negotiations will be secret, but Jimmy McGregor of Hong Kong's Chamber of Commerce believes that Hong Kongers can make their views felt:

> It is the two governments in London and Peking who will decide what happens to Hong Kong, but if the two governments concerned are aware of the strength of feeling of people that may have some influence on the way they decide to establish their policy or shape their policy towards negotiations. If the views of the people of Hong Kong are well known to both sides, then at least we start from a fairly realistic basis.

The Hong Kong government has taken no steps to canvass the views of its people on their future. They do not really need to; at least half the population—the immigrants from China—have voted with their feet in favour of Hong Kong, and as Jimmy McGregor puts it, 'there hasn't exactly been a problem of reverse immigration', so clearly the young generation of Hong Kongers aren't too keen on being reintegrated into China. If pushed, the older generation will probably accept a Chinese takeover—they have lived under the system before, however much they may have disliked it. The younger generation, on the other hand, feels it is a bind. Successive British immigration laws have made it clear that Britain will not take in the two and a half million 'British' passport holders in Hong Kong, and no other country has indicated a willingness to take that number of immigrants. Either a favourable solution can be found or they become People's Republic of China nationals willy-nilly. Naturally they are unhappy at this option. Christine Loh of the Hong Kong Observers led the chorus of demands for a say in the future of the colony in a letter to the *South China Morning Post* in July 1981:

> If we are not given any say in our future form of government we fear that the freedom of expression to which we have become accustomed

will be severely curtailed. We have all made some contribution towards Hong Kong's prosperity and we would like to continue to make our contribution to the society we live in, and we ask in return that our rights and feelings be considered. We sincerely feel that the interest and happiness of over five million people in Hong Kong can and should be accommodated by London and Peking.

It was a cry from the heart, but it got no response from government.

In a sense, groups like the Observers have already admitted the inevitable. Christine Loh concedes that

Hong Kong is part of Chinese territory and eventually it will be assimilated back into the Chinese system. I think I would not object to that because I'm ethnic Chinese and somehow I see the future of Hong Kong more with China than with Britain. But in twenty-five years' time I hope I can still enjoy relative freedom of expression, that I can live in a fairly liberal environment. What we want is that from 1997 to whenever, there should be a peaceful transition period, where the interests of the people of Hong Kong will be taken into account.

Finding out what the Chinese are going to do is a bit like looking through an out-of-focus telescope. Certain things can be vaguely discerned, but much of the detail is hazy. The essential fact of Hong Kong remains. It is the last product of the unequal treaties of the nineteenth century. The best official statement of the Chinese position was given in a letter from China to the United Nations Special Committee on Colonialism in 1972:

The questions of Hong Kong and Macau belong to the category of questions resulting from the series of unequal treaties which the imperialists imposed on China. Hong Kong and Macau are part of Chinese territory occupied by the British and Portuguese authorities. The settlement of the questions of Hong Kong and Macau is entirely within China's sovereign right and does not at all fall under the ordinary category of colonial territories. Consequently they should not be included in the list of colonial territories covered by the declaration on the granting of independence to colonial countries and people. With regard to the questions of Hong Kong and Macau, the Chinese government has consistently held that they should be settled in an appropriate way when conditions are ripe.

It is a long statement of position, but worth quoting as much for what it does not say as for what it does. Essentially the 1997 problem is left as one for Britain to deal with. Since China does not recognise the legality of the New Territories lease (or of the leases which gave Hong Kong island and Kowloon to Britain), the theoretical date for the end of the lease means nothing. Hong Kong can be reincorporated into China at any time China wishes. The diplomatic options are all China's. The option of independence

Hong Kong Harbour—China's gateway to the world.

is clearly ruled out. In China's eyes Hong Kong is not a colony to be given self-government.

One intriguing theory of China's view of the 1997 lease is thus that it does not really see the lease as having a date on it at all. This argument holds that 99 years—the original length of the lease—is in fact a devious Chinese way of saying 'for years and years', i.e. for ever. According to this optimistic school, China has no intention of doing anything about Hong Kong. That is a conclusion that one might arrive at from studying China's actions, as opposed to its words about Hong Kong.

The words have frequently been bellicose, the actions rarely so. In the early days, just after the British seizure of Hong Kong, the Chinese government made clear its intention to expel the barbarian as soon as possible. It proved impossible to do this and the matter of the return of Hong Kong, while it remained on the official agenda of the Chinese imperial government, went no further. The years of upheaval that followed the revolution of 1911 were hardly conducive to ending British rule over the colony: Britain was, until the Second World War, quite strong enough to prevent China from doing anything about Hong Kong. The collapse of British power in 1941, however, offered China an opportunity. The Nationalist government of Chiang Kai Shek announced on 16 August 1945, immediately after the capitulation of Japan, that it would accept the surrender of Hong Kong. British and Chinese forces raced each other to the island. The Americans had already assumed that China would take over

159

Hong Kong as part of the spoils of victory—China was, after all, an ally. After much hurried consultation between the governments of China, Britain and America, Chiang Kai Shek withdrew with grace, announcing that 'China would not send troops to accept the surrender of Hong Kong lest this should arouse allied misunderstanding'. But he expressed the hope that Britain and China might be able to negotiate a peaceful settlement to the Hong Kong 'problem'.

After the 1949 revolution the new communist government of China regarded the position in exactly the same light as its predecessors but, unlike its predecessors, was not bound by any constraints of alliance with Britain. As the communist armies, victorious in the civil war, began to roll towards Hong Kong, the colony's defences were strengthened and the British government stated that 'it was the intention of HM Government to maintain their position in Hong Kong'. The crisis blew over and Peking contented itself with denunciations of Britain as the 'oppressors of Chinese people' and as a 'challenge to the Chinese people which would lead to serious consequences'. Thereafter, there were regular border incidents and propaganda attacks on Britain, but it became clear that China did not intend a frontal attack on Hong Kong.

Delicate needling continued to remind Britain of its illegal position in Chinese eyes. In March 1952, after a serious fire in Hong Kong had wiped out some squatter villages, causing much distress, the communist authorities of Canton tried to send a 'comfort mission' to visit their brethren in the colony. The mission was turned back at the border and a skirmish ensued in which twelve people were injured, one of them dying subsequently. The Chinese press denounced this as 'pre-arranged slaughter'.

In 1966/7 during the Cultural Revolution it did look as if China intended to end the strange position of Hong Kong once and for all. Rioting spilled over into Hong Kong and the life of the colony was paralysed for months. There were frequent border incidents, including a pitched battle in the village of Sha Tau Kok. The voice of propaganda from Peking rose to a new pitch. In August 1967 the *People's Daily*, the Communist Party paper, reminded its readers that:

> More than a century ago British imperialism came to China by pirate ships, provoked the criminal opium war, massacred numerous Chinese people and occupied the Chinese territory of Hong Kong and the New Territories. This is an enormous blood debt British imperialism owes to the Chinese people. Sooner or later the Chinese people will make a thoroughgoing liquidation of this debt with British imperialism.

Over the years since then, while the language may have moderated somewhat, the basic position has not. Now that Hong Kong is playing so vital a role in the modernisation of China, its anachronistic position is almost as much of a burden to China as it is to Britain. Although an official of the Xinhua news agency did admit publicly in September 1978 that the riots of 1967 were 'a mistake', that is as far as China will be able to go in reversing its views on Hong Kong. The fundamentals remain the same however much the peripherals change.

They have changed enormously. The new openness of China means that Hong Kong is playing a vital role in 'turning Chinese cabbages into US dollars', as Financial Secretary John Bremridge puts it. Without Hong Kong's expertise the modernisation programme will founder. But those in Hong Kong who talk enthusiastically of the border 'withering' as Hong Kong and the Special Economic Zone of Shum Zhum become one are still living in cloud-cockoo land. Already the realities are making themselves felt again in mainland China.

The return to power of the 'revisionists' under the leadership of Deng Xiaoping has on the surface produced a new and stable regime. In the official words of one Chinese guide to trade in China, 'The party is at one with the people. The years of turmoil are over; wrongs have been set right. We can now dedicate ourselves to a bright future—the building of a powerful modern socialist nation.' Underneath the surface, not all is proceeding so smoothly. Recently Deng's attempts to liberalise certain aspects of the economy have come under attack from hardliners in China. The army has been concerned by his moves to give incentives to peasant farmers, as this has hit recruiting. It is also irritated by his attacks on the privileges of the elite, among which many army commanders are numbered. The state's bureaucrats have also resisted Deng's new policies, fearing that they will have to carry the can if they go wrong. It seems that China may be swinging again towards a more revolutionary hardline policy, one which will inevitably exclude considerations of the advantages of a place like Hong Kong. Despite the universal belief that the Cultural Revolution went too far, a recent article in the party's theoretical organ *Red Flag* noted that there was significant growth in the economy at that time, and criticism of Mao for launching the Red Guards on China has become steadily more muted in the last year.

These are straws in the wind, but in China a few straws always blow before the storm starts. There must be a real possibility of a change of policy which will see a more hostile line taken towards Hong Kong and its supposed special status with China. There is one factor which indicates not only that China has started thinking about the future of Hong Kong, but that it is thinking in the long term. Chinese officials have made frequent statements of the possible value of Hong Kong to China in strategic terms in the event of a major war with the Soviet Union. Hong Kong with its excellent port facilities and deepwater harbour would be, they say, an ideal place to offload war materials for China in the event of a Soviet attack. Such materials, they have hinted, should come from 'friendly' countries like Britain and the United States. The bonus of retaining Hong Kong as it is would be that the Russians would be reluctant to escalate any conflict with China by armed attacks against a third power—for such attacks, so runs the Chinese argument—would lead to retaliation on the part of Britain and the United States. In essence this sophisticated view sees Hong Kong, under British rule, as the ultimate Chinese defence against the Soviet Union. It is quite clear that China still regards the Soviet Union as the major threat.

Gateway to China

The third of China's lost sheep, after Hong Kong and Taiwan, is the Portuguese colony of Macau, fifty miles across the Pearl River from Hong Kong. Yet the strange story of Macau's attempts to return to the fold may be a pointer to the future of Hong Kong. Macau was the first European colony to be established in China, in 1557. For many years it was the centre of the China trade. By the beginning of the nineteenth century its vulnerability to attack and lack of a harbour made the merchants who lived there—by then overwhelmingly British—look for a safer port. They moved to Hong Kong and Macau went into a gentle decline, unnoticed by everyone else.

In the Cultural Revolution, Macau was invaded by Red Guards. They rampaged through the streets quite unchecked and hauled the Portuguese governor out of his mansion and harangued him in the street. The Portuguese government, aware that it could give no help, did the unexpected: it offered to return Macau to China. The Chinese were astonished and the Red Guards retired while China thought the offer over. It was turned down; the Chinese government felt that taking over Macau might have too destabilising an effect on Hong Kong, then as now their most important source of foreign exchange. Portuguese colonial authority was restored.

To keep the peace, Macau has made itself useful to everyone. For Hong Kongers, it has provided the one thing they cannot get in the colony—gambling. The Sociedade de Turismo e Diversoes de Macau runs several casinos (including a floating one) which have now become the backbone of Macau's economy. The STDM effectively runs the colony and is far and away its largest business. Appropriately, the STDM's chairman, Stanley Ho, has a magnificent house on the top of the hill in Macau—looking down on the governor's official palace.

Macau also services China. At its frontier with China, formalities are kept to a minimum and it is possible to meet someone from China on a bridge without either one of you leaving the country you have come from. This means that large numbers of businessmen come to Macau to do informal deals with Chinese contacts. The Portuguese have learned the Chinese art of pragmatism.

Macau, Portuguese toehold in China.

Further evidence that China is thinking seriously about the future of Hong Kong has come in recent statements about Taiwan, one of its other lost sheep. Taiwan is the island off the mainland to which the defeated nationalists under Chiang Kai Shek retired after the end of the civil war in 1949. Provided Taiwan agrees to reunification, the Chinese government has generously offered to let Taiwan retain considerable autonomy: its own armed services and economic system (capitalist like Hong Kong's), and its own laws and customs; Peking has also promised that foreign investment will be protected. In the eyes of many in Hong Kong, this is intended for the colony's consumption as well. K. M. Pang, a Chinese industrialist, regards this as a message to Hong Kong:

> This is typical Chinese you know; that when a father wants to tell the son something, he may not tell him directly, he may convey the message through the brother. This is what has happened in this statement to Taiwan, I think. I think we should plan towards that rather than hoping that Britain will stay and maintain the status quo.

Many people wonder if the preferred Chinese solution isn't going to be some sort of semi-autonomy under broad overall Chinese jurisdiction. One thing seems clear: that the British flag that flies over Hong Kong will have to be lowered, possibly only for a short time, possibly for ever. It is inconceivable, given Chinese history, that Britain will be allowed to continue its rule

163

indefinitely. One theory has it that Britain will formally lower the British flag and hand over the whole colony to China. China will then, out of consideration for the welfare of the Chinese people of Hong Kong and a desire not to disturb their way of life, let the whole place back to Britain again on a clear and mutually agreed length of lease. Thus essentially the British will become sub-contractors to the Chinese government, operating to masters in Peking rather than London.

If that does happen it won't be an untenable solution. Britain's essential interests in Hong Kong are, as they have always been, commercial. The British are no longer empire-builders—we have reverted to what we were before, a nation of shopkeepers. The fact that we happen to be quite good at running small places like Hong Kong should not blind us to the realities. It is not central to Great Britain's future that she should continue administering the economy and social services of a far-off Asian state. The possibility that Hong Kong might under Chinese overall control advance towards some form of representative local government—which is what an increasing proportion of the Hong Kong Chinese seem to want—is prevented at the moment only by the fact of British administration. Remove that and the Hong Kong Chinese could start shaping their own destiny, free of the threat of China or the dead hand of Britain. It would of course be a destiny within the overall framework of China.

Whatever happens in the future the great hope is that it will happen peacefully and with the willing co-operation of Hong Kongers. The chances are high that the transition, whatever form it takes, will be peaceful. Chinese pragmatism should ensure that. The tale is told of the Western missionary in China who received, in the course of a controversy, a particularly rude letter. He wrote back what he considered to be a polite but slightly sharp reply. Before sending it he showed it to a Chinese friend whose comment was 'You cannot send that letter, it will break off relations.' The missionary replied: 'I know that. But what else can I do?' The reply was brief and very Chinese: 'He is your neighbour. You have to go on living beside him.'

INDEX